I Gr
You Well

I Greet You Well

Mike Lawrence

Lewis Masonic

Dedication

For My Wife Debbie

Front cover: Photograph by Debbie Lawrence, with special thanks to W. Bro. D. Hollands and the Trustees of the Sandgate Masonic Centre.

First published 2018

ISBN 978 0 85318 549 9

Published by Lewis Masonic

an imprint of Ian Allan Publishing Ltd, Addlestone, Surrey KT15 2SF.

Printed in Malta.

Visit the Lewis Masonic website at www.lewismasonic.co.uk

Contents

About the Author

Past Master (Radnor Lodge No. 2587)
Past Zerubbabel (Temple Chapter No.558)
Cornwallis Lecturer 2009
Colin Dyer Memorial Lecturer 2010
Member of the East Kent Provincial Debating Team 2011

Having joined Freemasonry in 1994, Bro Lawrence progressed through the chair of his mother Lodge in 2000. His first Masonic article was published 1998 and he presented his first Masonic lecture in 2001. His portfolio now contains over 40 lectures which he has presented to the Provinces of South East England and the Metropolitan Grand Lodge. His lectures have raised over £10,000 for charity.

In 2008, he was greatly honoured to be appointed Provincial Assistant Grand Standard Bearer and in 2014, promoted to Past Provincial Deputy Grand Sword Bearer. In 2009, he was invited by the R. W. Bro Michael Robin Bailey, Provincial Grand Master for East Kent, to present the annual Cornwallis Lecture. In 2010, he was invited to give the Colin Dyer Memorial Lecture and in 2011, he participated as a member of the East Kent debating team. Also in 2011, to celebrate his 10th anniversary of Masonic lecturing, he produced several new lectures with unique musical themes from which all proceeds went to the East Kent 2014 Festival.

From 1997-2016, he was the manager of the Masonic Centre, Grace Hill, Folkestone.

In addition to his lectures, his work has been published in *Freemasonry Today*, *The Provincial* and at http://thefreemason.com. His short stories and articles have also appeared in several non-Masonic publications and periodicals and he continues to present regular Masonic articles through his own blog site, "Freemasons are us!" found at:

http://freemasonsareus.wordpress.com/

He is happily married to Debbie and enjoys an active family life with his children, grandchildren and great grandchildren.

Beneficiaries from the £10,000 raised through the lectures have been:

Fairlawn's Residential Centre for Children, Ashford.
Foxwood Special School, Hythe.
Macmillan Nurses.
Rhodes Minnis Cat Sanctuary.
Lord Whiskey Animal Sanctuary.
Canterbury Dogs Trust.
Help 4 Heroes.
Kent Masonic Library and Museum Trust
East Kent 2014 Festival
Mark Benevolent Fund
Royal Arch Bi-Centenary Appeal
Military Wives Choir Shorncliffe
Hythe Festival

Acknowledgements

I wish to acknowledge the following people that have supported and encouraged me to write and lecture over the last 20 years:

The late W. Bro Geoff Goode, who was instrumental in publishing my lectures in pamphlet form and who accompanied me on many lecturing engagements.

W. Bro Douglas Haynes JP, who invited me to present my first lecture at the Valley of Elham Lodge, during the millennium year.

The late W. Bro Bernard Cordell and the late W. Bro Rev Canon Leonard Tyzack, who prior to their deaths, presented me with their Masonic book collections as well as many other brethren who have presented me with Masonic books.

To the many brethren, too numerous to mention, who have listened respectfully to my lectures, asked relevant questions, shared interesting information and helped me raise over £10,000 for charity in the process.

To Suzanne Mills for her graphic editing assistance in the preparing and formatting of the illustrations.

To the immeasurable patience shown by my wife during the times when the dining room table had all but disappeared under books and papers and the office was awash with rough drafts.

Foreword

It has been 300 years since the formation of the first Grand Lodge of England and although that first century saw many challenges to its position and authority it managed to grow and find itself a position in England which has been the envy of many other societies. Peaking in popularity during the Victorian era and the early Edwardian years, it was the Second World War that saw the beginnings of its decline, culminating in a vitriolic campaign against it and the start of the general public believing it was a sinister and dark organisation.

High profile court cases of the sixties, seventies and eighties, that involved Freemasons, did not help and only encouraged governments, the judiciary, police and local authorities to seek out and identify Freemasons amongst its ranks. By the mid-nineties we almost saw an anti-Masonic campaign started by the Labour party, whose government of the day attempted to embarrass Grand Lodge by insisting it name all of its members. This was averted by the stance of Grand Lodge that claimed they were not in a position to make public the names of its members who had the civil liberty to be a member of any society that was neither illegal nor banned.

In any case, the members themselves were not in hiding and many of their names were published annually in Provincial year books, and membership lists for private clubs, which were already required by local authorities, were available. Besides this, no Lodge, whether it be Grand, Provincial or Private actually met in secret, as not only are many of their meetings publicly announced in various journals, but any member of the public can stand outside a Masonic meeting place and readily identify a Freemason from a hundred paces.

Fortunately, a crisis was averted and a new openness developed within the organisation and the past decade has seen a small but definite revival in the positive publicity Freemasonry now receives.

Yet though all of this, Freemasonry has continued to practice in all its forms, those two truly beautiful ornaments, namely beneficence and charity and have, in many cases without public awareness, raised millions of pounds for charity, and I would not be wrong in saying that monies raised in this way, have touched, in some form, every man, woman and child in the United Kingdom. As every year, millions of pounds are given to every type of good cause and charity that exists. From lifeboats to ambulances, from support groups to animal welfare sanctuaries, from hospices to hospitals, from babies to pensioners, from medical research to cures, from disasters to community projects, the list is endless. Yet so much of this is done in a quiet, unassuming manner, the public do not realise that every single Freemason in England makes personal contributions to good causes at every meeting they attend.

Then there are those Freemasons that play a role in many support groups, community initiatives, school councils, local councils and many other associations where people give their time freely to assist the community. In fact, in both these areas of giving time and money, Freemasons live the ethos of their organisation by offering brotherly love and relief to all, not just to Freemasons, ironically this in itself dispels that old outdated belief that Freemasons look after themselves.

During this time, membership has fluctuated and many Lodges have seen a slow decline in their members. This is not peculiar to Freemasonry, as all societies, fraternities and associations have reported a general decline in their membership and it is indicative of a general condition throughout the country in which men and women find more and more activities to take up their time and have moved away from the time honoured associations.

In trying to explain the unexplainable of how Freemasonry has outgrown its original prospect and become a worldwide organisation, much of this book takes its rise from the confusion of its humble origins in 1717. These uncertain beginnings have never been helped by the fact that so many Masonic scholars have attempted to explain away errors, which were inherited as fact. This coupled with the reverential awe and respect we all give to Freemasonry in general, probably brought on by much of the over exaggerated secrecy that has surrounded it all and in many cases purposely perpetuated by its members, has meant that there still exists today total confusion as to the true origin of the Craft and the possible belief that any such admissions as to a possible shady beginning, may in fact now be detrimental to the Craft.

But whatever our beginnings, whatever untruths are uncovered, whatever our ups and downs may be, this work merely lends itself to underpinning the very existence of our Fraternity and is in no way meant to be detrimental to the Craft, which these days is now beginning to out grown any suspicious nonsense, as most new theories of origin can be dismissed without too much thought. Whereas this book considers existing research and documents and places them in a new logical light, which above all is merely an idea and not a fact, and should be viewed as such.

This new light on old ideas theme was brought about by the many articles I have read that have been published by Quataur Coronati in their annual transactions. The articles have always received critical analysis from the members and in my experience are reliably researched and never based on unsubstantiated facts. The editorial team thoroughly vet each submission which are then presented to what could be considered as some of the greatest Masonic minds, who, in most cases are experts, authors and historians in their own right, with proven Masonic credentials. Their work has spanned the years and their research has unpicked the thread of unreliable facts that promulgated throughout Masonry during its first 150 years.

The shorter articles contained herein, some humorous, are merely observations of day to day Craft membership and practices.

I have also tended to steer away from spiritual explanations, which in my own mind should never have been allowed to infiltrate the Craft. These spiritual rationalisations have tended to divert our thoughts and detract from our science, particularly when we read such nonsense as published in a book entitled *Occult Powers,* which described the Masonic journey as being *"Divided into the three degrees of Apprentice, Journeyman or Fellowcraft and Master...the author presents a comprehensive textbook in developing your occult knowledge.... The reader is lead to soul-searching through instructions that connect the yogic systems...the physiological and physic... in implementing higher exercises to learn the power of the Od...the apprentice exercise will give vital energy...the journeyman exercise helps us experience telepathy, higher breathing techniques, idealistic monism, dreams, clairvoyance and clairaudience, and the healing power of magnetism...in the final development stage the reader is given the last key to see all things through the inner eye and thus become a master."*

Personally, and I say this with all due respect to the writer, this type of work is not Masonic, and to associate the Craft with the occult is both damaging and detrimental and will leave us open to ridicule and condemnation. It will do no more that perpetuate the general public view of Freemasonry, thinking we are a strange sect, and those of us at the forefront of speaking to the public in general about Freemasonry will, without a doubt, understand exactly what I am saying.

This is one of the reasons that led me, over the last 20 years, to start writing and lecturing about Freemasonry, my main reason being to help brethren get a better understanding of what they are doing. I have attempted to bring logic and plain speaking into our somewhat simple Craft. For despite, what you might have read, Freemasonry is simple in its approach, it practices and its usages. I agree that to many, this is not the case and they continue to produce reams of work, which takes some theories to the nth degree of explanation and all in the most eloquent and plausible terms. Thus, convincing us we have possible missed something in our daily advancement or losing out because we have not read the latest book.

One such example is our allegorical association with King Solomon's Temple. This as we know was introduced by our ritual writers around the 1725 period, and was first found in that most popular exposure of the time, *Masonry Dissected*, by Samuel Pritchard. The story was the imagination of somebody who while wishing to accentuate a salient point in our ritual thought it a good idea to invent something. Most of our ritual then followed the same suit, with the proviso that all what we were being taught was allegory and that is where the problem starts, well-meaning brethren sought to prove that allegory, which is a paradox in itself. Ultimately thousands upon thousands of man-hours have been devoted to proving the unprovable, resulting in total confusion, thus we now have a Craft membership that believe our ritual association with King Solomon and the building of his Temple, is historically correct in every particular.

Therefore, we have arrived at a situation where in many cases, and through lack of personal study and any official guidance, we have reached a stage where we have indoctrinated our own membership with incorrect and inaccurate facts without actually trying and by allowing so called Masonic authors to publish the most romantic and fanciful unfounded ideas, we continue to perpetuate the myths.

Is it because Freemasonry is a money-spinner or big business, you might well ask? Whatever the case, I think it a pretty poor show that people are allowed to exploit a group of men that already pay their hard-earned cash for membership fees and charitable contributions. But that's another story, least to say we need to be much more discerning in our reading material. However, I cannot apologise for my candid views as they have been tried and tested, readily received and positively encourages by the thousands of Brethren and hundreds of Lodges that have enjoyed my lectures and help raise over £10,000 for charities and good causes.

It was by utter fluke that I have found myself in a position at this time to consider publishing a book of my papers, lectures and writings which I hope will shed some light on certain subjects and give a better understanding of others. Needless to say, I do not expect you to agree with everything I write, but good discourse must start somewhere and existing truths or proven documents is a good starting point rather than wordy speculation, spurious rumours and unsubstantiated facts.

To progress as a fraternity, we must always challenge convention. Not to be detrimental or to denigrate the Craft, but to seek knowledge of why things are so, the truth behind what we practice, to understand our usages and to build a firm and unshakable foundation that will last even longer. Freemasonry is not a mystery and it is not secret, it merely practices traditions which only its members are subject to. After all, a football coach does not reveal his game plan, an entrepreneur his business plan nor a successful author the plot of his new book. However, if you are a team member, a business financier or buy the author's book, everything is revealed to you.

On that thought, thank you for purchasing this book and I only hope you enjoy reading the articles just as I have enjoyed writing them.

M.L.
Folkestone
January 2018

Examining the development of Accepted Masonry, its Ritual and the influences and contribution made by Operative masonry to the Craft

Stealing History

(Written in 2000)

When the Angles and the Saxons first came to ancient Britain, they initially maintained a form of military organisation at each settlement, but as time passed and settlements became villages a civil form of social order began to evolve. Beginning with blood-kin, they came together for mutual protection and support, developing in time, community ties that replaced the blood relationship. This brought order to the settlement and protection for the individual against the group. These associations, often described as artificial as opposed to the bond of blood, were the natural development of a group of people with social needs. Exactly as centuries before when the Greeks had their *"thiassoi"* and the Romans with their *"collegia"* both of which we could say developed in response to social necessity.

Throughout Europe, associations of likeminded people became so popular they covered every conceivable purpose: for eating, for drinking, ensuring a decent burial, for worship, for hunting, for banking. There were organisations for sailors, travellers, woodsmen, shepherds, women, children, rich, poor, town dwellers and country folk and so on. They ran armies, schools, hospitals and all those practices and industries that go to make up the social organisation of a community.

People following the same craft or trade also began to make these informal arrangements amongst themselves to regulate competition and keep their professional standards high. Every form of work, craft or type of trade thus became organised into a group. In England during the middle-ages, it became the practice to call such a group or association names like "company", "corporation" "fellowship" or "mystery" known to us today by the term "Guild", we can safely say they were not invented but rather grew out of natural conditions.

This meant that in any town, city or district, men from each trade or craft had an organisation of their own. They had rules, regulations and officers. They admitted members on oath, tried members guilty of violating the rules, and punished them by fines or expulsion. They trained apprentices and held a monopoly on their own kind of trade. They had prayers for the dead, relief for widows and orphans. They also had a patron Saint and feast days.

In England, each Master of a trade was allowed two apprentices and a list was made of waiting applicants on which their particulars were entered. Hence the possible origins of the term *"Entered Apprentice"*. After they had served their time, generally seven years, they became a journeyman and became eligible, in their own right, to join their Fellowship and were known as a fellow of the Craft, hence the origins of the term 'Fellow-Craft'.

Here are some examples of working ways of the early trade fellowships:

In 1365, John Russell, a poulterer was charged with exposing 37 pigeons for sale, that were putrid, rotten, stinking and abominable to the human race; to the scandal, contempt and disgrace of the City and his Gild. He was sentenced, by his Fellowship, to the pillory and the said pigeons were burnt under him.

In 1531, the Wardens of the Coopers Fellowship were empowered to seize any defective cask and to amend or burn them, while the maker was to be fined.

In 1511, the Loriners who had strict quality controls from their ordinances of 1261, complained to the Mayor and Aldermen about the importation of sub-standard French bits (part of the horse's bridal).

The 13 loaves of the "Baker's Dozen" were derived from the early days of strict Fellowship regulations about bad quality and weight.

As these illustrate, the Fellowships protected customers, employers and employees alike.

Most of these trade associations were small, the largest one being the Corpus Christi Gild at York recorded as having some 1,500 members. Occasionally they would merge, but not those in the City of London. Because of their close association with the church, many participated in pageants and in mystery, morality and miracle plays. These were staged on wagons and drawn in procession through the streets of the town. In Norwich for example, the Mercers, Drapers and Haberdashers presented *"the creation"*. The Grocers, *"Paradise"* and the Smiths, *"David and Goliath."* While at Hereford, the Glovers depicted *"Adam and Eve,"* the Carpenters *"Noah's Ark"* and the Tailors *"the Three Kings"*.

Perhaps it is not too far from the imagination to consider that some Masonic legend could well have originally developed from an old mystery play which found its way through some stonemason's fellowship that enacted the building of *"King Solomon's Temple"*.

It may also be worthy of a mention at this stage that many of these associations, accepted men not engaged in their particular craft as patrons or as a means of bestowing an honour or special privilege. It can be said that many members of London Companies frequently came to have only a very faint connection with the business of the Company to which they were attached. They included in their membership most of the wealthy men of the nation. Royal patronage was also not uncommon as Edward III, Henry IV, Henry VI and Henry VIII were all honorary members of Fellowships.

Although during this time there was no one national organisation to federate the various local guilds, the civil laws which governed them were the same everywhere as were the methods of training apprentices. It can therefore be said that each trade throughout England was accepted as a single profession. Consequently, a workman could move from one place to another with the expectation of becoming a member of the local trade fraternity. Members of the builder's trade or craft were highly skilled and educated men. It is not an exaggeration to say that they were the ablest of men the Middle Ages produced. During a period of some 200 years they designed and constructed some 1,700 cathedrals and thousands of chapels, monasteries, castles, fortresses and halls. Not many of them could actually read or write, but their own apprenticeship, in what was considered the greatest of the arts, was so thorough, and they together possessed among themselves so large a body of knowledge, that a Master of this trade was considered more educated than a Bishop.

This intimacy with each building meant that they knew both the weakest and the strong points of any structure, plus any escape tunnels, secret passages and "hidey" holes. Therefore, their allegiance would be of great benefit to any King. With the principles of the Gothic cathedral, which were their discovery, and their art which was their monopoly, they were able to produce a building which was unequalled in the past by no other architecture except the Greek, and has yet to be surpassed.

In England, the Saxons built structures mainly of wood, some of which were recorded in the Domesday book in 1086. However, few still remain. The Saxons could carve stones, i.e. crosses and memorials, but they were not really masons in the sense of builders in stone. With the coming of the Normans, things changed. They brought to these shores the technique of Roman vaulting as a means of roofing our cathedrals and churches, achieving breath-taking effects with carved stonework, the like of which had never been seen.

Towards the end of the 12th century great religious foundations began to appear and since there were very little or no practical expert builders in stone in this country at that time, Master Masons were brought into the country, from France. The first Gothic building being the monastery church of St Denis, erected near Paris in 1140. The building of a cathedral or any other great work of architecture always followed a set procedure. A foundation or administration authority was set up to furnish the money and to act as employer. It chose a Superintendent or Chief Master Mason. The Master Mason, sometimes called the Master of the Fabric or Master of the Work, was responsible for the hiring and firing of workmen, quantifying the materials, making the plans and overseeing the architectural details. The Office of Master was one of great dignity for which he annually received gloves, a robe and monies all in addition to his daily allowance.

When the workers arrived they often slept in their Lodge or occasionally a village of houses were built for them. The men were organised under the leadership of the Chief Master Mason who was assisted by other officers. At every site, a shed or cabin, was erected for their headquarters and became known as a Lodge. It is interesting to note that the term *"loge"*, is of French Gallic origin. The Lodge was set up close to the south wall of the intended building and had windows in the east, south and west sides, mainly to take advantage of the sun light. It was here that meetings were held as often as the work required, to enforce discipline and to receive instructions. It was also used as a workshop and to house tools and supplies and was equipped with tracing boards for plans. Some of the craftsmen had servants and helpers and labourers were also engaged, as were other local trades. These, however were not allowed to join the in any of the meetings. Neither were they permitted to learn the mysteries of the art nor receive the same pay or privileges.

The word mystery is derived from the Latin word *"ministerium"* meaning professional skill. It does not refer to mysteries in the sense of secrets.

An important point to consider here is that generally speaking, the buildings were isolated and cut off from outside forms of amusement. Therefore, they tended to keep themselves in tight little communities and were probably looked upon by the locals as suspicious foreigners. During the summer months, they would compete in sports like archery, wrestling, running and fishing, but during the winter they would probably use the Lodge as a club room. It has been suggested that the origin of the lectures emanated from the long winter evenings when the Masons sought to increase their knowledge amid the fellowship of the fraternity and while partaking of refreshment. On the completion of the building, the temporary hut was dismantled or put to other purposes. The craftsmen disbanded to seek work elsewhere. Of course, some buildings were so vast that a craftsman might spend his entire working life on one project. This practice continued until about the middle of the 16th century when it is generally believed that a Lodge was maintained for its own sake, by non-operatives. Certainly, it would appear and records suggest that by the 1590s, the Gentry and Freemen of the town were received into some sort of Operative Lodge by Acception, and maintained that association without the involvement of skilled Masons.

These new Lodges began to develop in three new directions:

1) Civil law required that such a body of men should have a Charter empowering it to work or exist. This requirement stood for every Gild or fraternity. To comply with this, Masons declared that in the 10th century their Craft had been granted a Royal Charter at York. They entered a written claim to this as their authorisation and appended it to a statement of their purposes and a set of their rules and regulations.

2) Where the temporary Lodge had existed as a means to an end and was focused on the construction work that was to be done. The permanent Lodge was focused on itself, the group members and possibly some non-political ethos.

3) Though the majority of its members long continued to be Operative Masons, they admitted or accepted, into their membership, a number of men who were not working masons.

These Lodges continued to work as centres throughout England, each one being independent of the others, yet it may appear understood they were not the only Lodge. This *ad hoc* type development continued until the early decades of the 18th century, at which time it has been suggested that there was probably some 200 of them. Some having a membership wholly composed of working or Operative Masons, some composed solely of Accepted Masons and some of mixed membership. In 1717, four London Lodges set up a Grand Lodge to be the centre of their activities in the Westminster area, but from this, each and every regular and duly constituted Grand Lodge in the world has descended.

Having given a thumbnail sketch of the rise of the Trade Fraternity, let us look at the possible influence the Operative trade had on Grand Lodge. Here I have chosen to present the history of Operative Masonry as recorded in the Old Manuscripts or Old Charges. There are over a 100 hand written copies of these ancient Manuscripts (MSs) written between the 15th and 18th centuries. These ancient MSs were used by the Medieval Trade associations of our Operative cousins, along with their Charters, to form the authority under which they worked and assembled.

You will note that the history which I am about to share with you does not include the Hiramic Legends, which as I will demonstrate later was formulated by exponents of our Speculative Art and not something that has been handed down since time immemorial. Additionally, the phraseology that I use in this section is in keeping with the terms written in the MS.

The history starts a little before the time of Noah, approximately 3000 BC, and describes the discovery of the seven Liberal Arts and Sciences by the three sons and daughter of Lamech. You can read this in Genesis 4: 18-22. It was these four children who founded all the Crafts of the world and they knew that God was about to take vengeance on the world because of the sin he saw, and they knew it would be by fire or water. Therefore, they inscribed these Sciences on two great pillars, one made of marble that fire would not burn and the other of lateres, which would not sink in the flood. Of the Seven Liberal Arts and Sciences, six rely on Geometry, this being the measure of the earth. *"Geo"* as in earth and *"metry"* as in measure. The Matthew Cooke MS *c.*1450 explains it thus:

> *"No handicraft that is wrought by mans hand but it is wrought by Geometry, and a notable cause, for if a man work with his hands he worketh with some manner of tool, and there is none instrument, of material things, in this world but it comes of the kind of earth, and to earth it will turn again, and there is none instrument, that is to say a tool to work with, but it hath some proportion, more or less. And proportion is measure, the tool, or the instrument, is earth. And Geometry is said to be the measure of the earth, wherefore, I may say that men live all by*

Geometry, for all men here in this world live by the labour of their hands."

An interesting analogy, but more important is the intricate weaving of the mystery of Geometry into the lore of the Operative Craft. The Bible tells us that a great flood did occur and the MS tell us that the two pillars were found when the waters subsided, the first by Pythagoras and the second by Hermes the philosopher. Both begun to expound the teachings of the Seven Liberal Sciences, but it was Hermes who taught Nimrod the art of measures, who in turn taught his workmen the craft of measures so as to build the Tower of Babel.

And Nimrod we are told, was made a Mason and he loved the Craft of Masonry very well. And he sent 40,000 Masons to build the city of Nineveh and other cities. And he gave a charge to each of those Masons that they should be true to each other and that they should live truly together. And they should serve their Lord and Master all their days that the Master should have all that belongs to him. He gave them other charges which was the first time that ever a Mason had any charge of his Craft.

The MS go on to tell us that when Abraham went down into Egypt, he taught there the Liberal Sciences and he had a worthy clerk named Euclid. The Legendary connection of Euclid with Masonry is referred to in the Masonic Lectures, 2nd Lecture, 2nd Section. Here we read that a Masonic Lodge was held at Alexandria where Euclid presided. The Cooke MS *c.*1450 states that he was a pupil of Abraham and learnt from him the Science of Geometry. However, history shows us the Euclid lived about 300 BC, while Abraham lived about 1900 BC. Here is the first true example of how the authors or writers of our history, introduced fictional or romantic imaginations, or better still allegory, to illustrate salient points or to emphasise certain aspects of history, purely to give it more impact.

The MS go on to tell us that Euclid knew the Seven Liberal Sciences right well and he was commissioned by the Kings and Lords of the Land to teach their sons the art of geometry that they might live honestly as Gentlemen. He taught them to build Churches, Castles, Towers, Manors and all sorts of other buildings and gave them the following charges:

1) That they should be true to the King which they serve.
2) To Elect the wisest and most cunning (skilful) of them to be Master of the Work.
3) That they should not love money.

4) That they should not employ "loses" which would bring shame on the Lodge. (The Melrose MS c.1674 describes the term "loses" as a man who had not completed a lawful apprenticeship.)
5) That they should assembly once a year to determine how best they may serve their Lord for his profit and their own credit.
6) That they correct within themselves those who have trespassed against the Craft.

Upon receiving these charges, they swore a great Oath and in return, they received reasonable pay that they might live honestly. And here was the Craft called Geometry and now throughout the world it is called Masonry.

The next part deals with the building of King Solomon's Temple and we are told that the King's Son of Tyre, was the Master Mason, and Solomon we are told, confirmed the Charges that David had given to Masons. Solomon himself taught them their manners with little difference to the manners that are now used.

Now by chance there was a cunning man named Naymus Graecus, a curious Craftsman, who was a contemporary of King Solomon and Charles Martel. The legend as set out in the ancient MS known as Grand Lodge MS, No 1 dated 1583, and tells us how Naymus Graecus goes to France to teach Charles Martel, this great and noble science.

Subsequent MS reproduce the legend, but with many variants in the spelling of the name. Charles Martel, known as Charles the Hammer, was born 688 and died 741. He is remembered for his defeat of the Saracens at Poitiers in 732 which saved Europe from being overrun by the Moslems. It is claimed in some of the Old Charges that he was a Patron of Masons. As previously stated, in legend and fable there is no chronological sequence therefore you have peoples brought together from different times purely to illustrate a point.

England at that time stood void as for any Charge concerning Masons until St Alban's time. The Cooke MS tells us:

"In his time the King of England who was a pagan did wall the town now called St Albans. St Alban was a worthy Knight & Steward of the Kings household, Governour of the Realme, & Overseer of the erecting of the walls of the town, a lover of Masonry & a cherisher of Masons; he made their pay right,

as the realme stood then, he gave three and sixpence a week to each Mason & threepence for their noon lunches. And always before that time Masons through all the Realm had noe more than a penny a day & night until St Alban mended it. He got a Charter from the King and Councel to hold a general Asembly to make Masons, and gave the Charge as you shall hear afterwards"

The fullest account of St Alban's legendary connection with Freemasonry can be found in the William Watson MS dated 1687. From St Alban, we leap to Athelston who was the King of England in 925-941AD. In the legend of the Craft it is said that he granted a Charter to the Masons to hold an Assembly every year. The first being held by his son Prince Edwin, at York in 926. This Charter being the one that the Operatives claimed was granted to them thereby enabling them to satisfy the Civil Law, and that is where we end the classic Operative history as told in the MSs.

So where are we at present? I have spoken about the growth of the trade or Gild system and how they could have developed into this Speculative Fraternity of ours. I have also looked at the age-old Craft of Operative Masons, their Charges and their legends. We have looked at how the first Speculative Lodges may have come about. What we cannot dispute is that some form of Fraternity, with its rules, regulations, and charges existed in medieval England.

What we do know is that:

1) That in England, certainly from 1560, a version of the MS Constitutions of Masonry was read to the candidate, who had to swear to keep the charges.
2) In Scotland, certainly from 1696, the Mason Word, with all that it implied, was imparted to candidates joining the Trade.
3) In England, Freemen or members of the Gentry joined the fraternity by Acception by about 1590.
4) In Scotland, non-operative or gentlemen masons were admitted to Lodges as early as 1600.
5) There is evidence to suggest that English Operative or Accepted Masons made use of secret modes of recognition by about 1650.
6) The Charges in general of the old MS Constitution of Masonry as dated from the 14th century, contained various

moral precepts, in addition to numerous trade regulations. There does not appear to be any attempt to veil the morality in allegory or to illustrate it by symbols.

Summarising the state of English Freemasonry at this point is essential to the development of the lecture and at this stage we have seen how the Gothic Architects and builders of the 12th century came to England at the behest of our great religious foundations to build our great cathedrals. That, as a result of this and influenced by medieval trade practices at the time, fraternities and fellowships were formed. We have much evidence of their practices and the great store they place on their *"mysteries"* or professional skills. From this we receive by way of their old manuscripts; trade practices, moral guidelines and their legends. We learn how the site hut or *"loge,"* became the most important place on the building site and how this developed into a permanent meeting place for groups of stone workers and by the 17th century, Accepted or Gentleman members were allowed to join.

But at this stage, there are two other important elements of development which affected Masonry. The first is the Mason Word which appears to originate in Scotland and of which it has been said throws more light on the origins of our present ceremonies than any of the early Craft MS. The second is the ritual or ceremony employed by Lodges to admit members. Looking at the former, what we must first ask is what was the point of obtaining or receiving such a word?

It was first and foremost not to demonstrate so much the skill of the person who was in possession of it, but more to show he had been trained in accordance with the rules of the organisation which guarded it, that he accepted those rules, and that he was entitled, on account of his membership of the organisation, to certain privileges in the matters of employment and relief. The need for some sort of secret mode of recognition among Masons arose from two specific problems that were peculiar to Scotland.

1) The first was that there was plenty of stone readily available for building and plenty of stone workers, but few really skilled workers owing to the scarcity of freestone which was capable of being carved. As a consequence, a test of skill would hardly suffice to distinguish masons from semi-qualified or unqualified stone workers, such as Cowan's.

In 1707, Kilwinning Lodge described a Cowan as a Mason without the Word, but we know the word Cowan more to mean dry dyker or builder of dry stone walls, although it went on to be used in a derogatory term used to describe a person who did the work of a Mason without having had the training.

2) The second point was to establish the difference between an Apprentice and a Fellowcraft or Journeyman. Tradesmen have, and always will, jealously guard their own skill or trade and the Mason Word was a privilege associated with the termination of an Apprenticeship and/or the admission to a Fellowship.

This of course begs the question of whether or not Apprentices, who were not qualified, nor Freemen, and therefore did not travel alone from job to job, were ever given or entrusted with a Word, even though the Apprentice was a grade accepted by the fellowship. Therefore, for an Apprentice to receive or be entrusted with such a Word would suggest that he was in fact more than that of a novice worker. Records in fact show us that there was a system of two classes or grades of Apprentice. The Schaw Statutes of 1598 and 1599 show that Apprentices were more likely to be the lowly young lad that started life as the errand boy etc, and the Entered Apprentice having completed his seven years, works as a journeyman to his Master before becoming a Fellow of the Craft.

Technicalities I am afraid, that must be passed over at this stage. Suffice to say that there was a Mason Word, which as I explained was peculiar to Operative Masons in Scotland and the very north of England, but ultimately influenced the Accepted Masons of the South.

The next question that begs to be answered is what could such a word have been. First, let me refer you to the VSL, The Gospel of St John Chapter 1:1.

> *"In the beginning was the Word, and the word was with God, and the Word was God."*

The Bible describes the "Word" as being God, and this possible interpretation is not surprising as the Operative Fellowships had, as we know, strong religious affiliations. Let me also say that this Mason Word may not have been spoken, but passed on by signs. This points me to those words repeated by the Principal Sojourner when asked to reveal the discovery of great importance found on the plate of gold by the Most Excellent Zerubbabel:

> *"That Most Excellent, we must humbly beg to decline, for we*

have heard with our ears, and our fathers have declared unto us, that in their days and the old time before them it was not lawful for anyone to pronounce the name of the True and Living God Most High, save the High Priest, nor him but once a year, when he entered the Holy of Holies and stood before the Ark of the Covenant to make propitiations for the sins of the people."

I use this example from an historical standpoint and not chronological, but from this we now learn that the name of the True and Living God Most High must never be spoken.

The two earliest references to what the Word may have been, and as far as I can ascertain both belong to 1725. One is contained is a skit or sketch concerning Masonry and the other occurs in the Masonic catechism – The Whole Institutions of Free-Masons Opened – both however say the same thing:

"Yet for all this I want the primitive word, I answered it was god...to wit I am, and jehova is the answered to it, and grip at the rein of the back, or else Excellent and Excellent, Excellency is the Answered to it, and grip as foresaid......"

From this we can guess that the Mason Word was probably the name of the True and Living God Most High, although the legend of its loss and subsequent discovery was not developed until well into the 18th century.

Looking at our early ritual, there can be little doubt that the old Charges present us with details of the ceremony or ritual of admission, and was as follows:

Firstly, A Prayer or Invocation was offered in this manner:

"The might of the Father of Heaven, with the might of his Son, and the goodness of the Holy Ghost be with us & our beginning, and send us good life, that we may come to his blessed Kingdom that never shall have end. Amen."

Secondly, came reading of the Legendary History, much of which you have heard this evening. This would commence in this manner:

"Good Brethren and Fellow's our purpose is to tell you how the worthy Science of Masonry first begun"

Thirdly, the holding out of the VSL for the candidate to place his hand on while a copy of the Charges was read to him and commence thus:

"Now will I rehears other things singular for Masons, for Maisters and Fellows"

Last came the Obligation, again while the candidate held the VSL and would begin:

"These Charges that wee have nowe rehearsed vnto yow all and all others that belong to Masons yee shall keepe. So healpe yow god..."

Unfortunately, the first references we have as to how the proceedings went is from the exposure of 1723 entitled *'The Mason's Examination'* and *"The Grand Whimsy"* an exposure of 1730. However, as previously mentioned, I can only touch on this subject briefly, but I am writing a more detailed lecture on the development of our ritual.

There is a great debate as to the number of grades or ceremonies there were, they were not known as degrees until 1730 and students have long since argued that there was one ceremony used for all grades and some argue two, here is some of the evidence cited.

Exponents of the one degree theory logically conclude that although there were three classes of Masons:

- Masters: Men who made contracts and undertook the work of building for employers.
- Fellow Crafts or Journeymen: Employed by these Masters to carry out the work.
- Entered Apprentices: Who were received that they might be taught the art of building.

The difference in rank did not involve any difference in the esoteric teaching. There was but one ceremony and one set of secrets. They cite the Schaw statutes of 1598 which says:

"...na maister or fellow of craft be...admittit without the number of sex maisters and twa enterit prenteissis, the wardene of that lodge being one of the said sex..."

It is believed that if two apprentices were to be present at the reception of a fellow-craft or master, there could have been no secrets to be communicated that the apprentices did not already know and were in possession of.

With regard to the Two Degree exponent's, let me here quote from the Prestonian Lecture given by Douglas Knoop in the late thirties in which he states:

> *"Reverting to our MS, which are the following...The Edinburgh Register House MS 1696, The Sloane MS. 3329. c.1700, The Trinity College, Dublin MS 1711,The Graham MS 1726, it may be noted that at the conclusion of what may be described as the ceremony, the word was circulated amongst those present and was finally given to the candidate by the Master. These signs and words were those of an entered apprentice, and, as the MS points out, there were others belonging to a master or fellowcraft, which were imparted as follows:*
>
> *First, all apprentices were ordered out of the company and none suffered to stay but masters. Then 'he who is to be admitted a member of fellowship' knelt and took an oath of secrecy, after which he went out with the youngest master to learn 'the posture and signes of the fellowship'. On returning, he made the master's sign and said the former words of entry, but leaving out the 'common judge'; the masons then whispered the word among themselves, and finally the master gave him the word and the grip. There is nothing in the said MS as to the nature of the master's sign, word or grip, though some indications are given regarding the apprentice's secrets.*
>
> *The fact that in 1696 there were two distinct ceremonies, if they may be so described, one applying to entered apprentices and one to fellow-crafts or masters."*

There would appear to be a distinct difference between English and Scottish Masonry at the time, with one and two grades respectively. What we do know is that of the two grades heretofore mentioned, the five points of fellowship was part of that esoteric knowledge that was passed to the candidates in those ceremonies; however, it did not have the Hiramic legend associated with it.

We can be quite sure that by about 1720 there was a trigradal system, with three sets of esoteric knowledge, words and signs. Both the Trinity

College, Dublin MS 1711 and The Graham MS 1726 suggest three ceremonies.

The Graham MS indicates a threefold scheme, Entering, Passing and Raising (This was usually referred to as being passed. The term raised was not introduced until 1738. Which gives more credence to the theory that the Hiramic legend had not fully developed) The Graham MS appears to be similar to that observed by Grand Lodge in 1723 which recognised three categories of Masons, each so far as one can tell with its own esoteric knowledge. These were, Apprentices, Fellow-crafts and Master of the Lodge.

The Trinity College, Dublin MS 1711 refers to, Entered Apprentices, Fellow Craftsman and Masters.

Prichard's Masonry Dissected 1730, describes, The Entered Prentice Degree, The Fellow Crafts Degree and The Masters Degree.

Other early references to this Trigradal System can be found in The Book of Fundamental Constitutions and the Orders of the Philo-Musicae et Architecturae Societas from which we learn that certain persons were Made Masons, Passed Fellow Crafts and Passed Masters in London in 1725.

As a final part to this section we must consider the following, the Trinity College, Dublin MS 1711, contains the following details regarding words and postures:

> "The Masters sign is back bone and the word matchpin. The fellow craftsman's sign is knuckles & sinues ye word Jackquin. The Enter-prentice's sign is sinues, the word Boaz or its hollow. Squeese the Master by ye back bone, put your knee between his, & say Matchpin. Squeese the fellow craftman in knuckles, and sinues & say Jackquin. squees the enterprentice in sinues & say boaz or its hollow."

I have this evening, touched very briefly of four subjects:
- The Trade Fellowships
- The Old Charges or MS
- The Mason Word
- The Evolution of our Ritual and Ceremony

Each, in its own right, could have complete volumes written about it. For my own part, all I have done this evening is to draw together various threads of information which are, through research, available to us all and I would encourage everyone to remember the Charge they received on the night of their initiation into Freemasonry where we were told:

> *"....without neglecting the ordinary duties of your station, to endeavour to make a daily advancement in Masonic knowledge."*

But to return to the title of this lecture – Stealing History – We have examined tonight how Operative Masonry developed through the Medieval Trade Systems, we can witness the change as Accepted Masons began to join in the late 16th and 17th centuries and ultimately take over existing Operative Lodges by the turn of the 18th century. So much so that in London, the Operative Masons who belonged to the fellowship of the Company of Masons would seem to have had little or no influence over those four old Lodges. In fact, Edwin Strong Snr, who alludes to the fact that he laid the last stone on the dome of St Paul's Cathedral, wrote this in 1707:

> *"Yet still in the South, the lodges were more and more disused, partly by the neglect of the Masters and Wardens and partly by not having a Noble Grand Master in London, and the annual assembly was not duly attended.....yet the old lodge near St Paul's, and a few more, continued their stated meetings."*

The "old Lodge near St Paul's", mentioned by Strong, has great significance. It was here, at the Goose and Gridiron, St Paul's Churchyard, that the first assembly of the Grand Lodge of England or Premier Grand Lodge of the World was held on 24 June 1717.

There were in fact, four Lodges which came together to form that first Grand Lodge:

> No 1 which met at the Goose and Gridiron, St Paul's Churchyard.
>
> No 2 which met at the Crown Ale-house, Parker's Lane, near Drury Lane.
>
> No 3 which met at the Apple Tree Tavern, Charles Street, Covent Garden.
>
> No 4 which met at the Rumner and Grapes, Channel Row, Westminster.

Unfortunately, the minutes of Grand Lodge only commence on 24 June

1723 and for its history, we are mainly dependent on an account given by Dr Anderson in the Constitutions of 1738:

> *"King George I. entered London most magnificently on 20 September 1714. And after the rebellion was over AD1716, a few Lodges at London finding themselves neglected by Sir Christopher Wren............"*

Clear evidence that Operative Lodges were falling into disuse. I therefore consider that it was the Accepted Masons of London who formed the Premier Grand Lodge for the Westminster area, and stole the principles of Operative Freemasonry and set themselves up as an order specifically for Accepted Masons.

In his book, *Symbols of Freemasonry*, Daniel Beresniak explains it in the following manner:

> *"Contrary to an old belief, which has been defended by many historians in the past, we are now in a position to demonstrate that Speculative Freemasonry did not derive directly from Operative Freemasonry. In the seventeenth and eighteenth centuries, Freemasons took their inspiration from the rites and customs of the Guild of Masons in order to give their work the structure, organisation and symbols necessary to fulfil a specific purpose. This was to gather together people of different origins and different opinions and enable them to work on a common project: the creation of a Temple for the whole of humanity.*
>
> *Rather than saying that Freemasonry was born out of the Guild of Masons, it might be more helpful to say that learned men who wished to work together and exchange ideas adopted the symbolism and structures used by working masons."*

It is not therefore surprising that the Grand Lodge seal used today is made up of two parts, half being the seal of the Company of Masons, a copy of which I attach as an appendix to the Lecture.

And finally if we take the fact that Grand Lodge do not recognise any formal Masonic organisation prior to the formation of the Premier Grand Lodge in 1717, we can only arrive at one conclusion: I firmly believe that the Ancient Fraternity of Free and Accepted Masons was formed by and for Gentleman and influenced heavily by Dr James Anderson, who having been expelled from St Pauls Operative Lodge in 1715, conceived a system of pure Speculative Freemasonry for Gentlemen in London who did not work at the trade, stealing the complete history of the Operative Fraternity in the process.

References / sources
1) E. R. Whitfield, *The Evolution of the Second and Third Degrees*
2) Robert Freke Gould, *The History of Freemasonry*
3) Gordon Christie, *Freemasonry as I see it*
4) B. A. Swindon, *The Evolution of the Masonic Lectures*
5) Daniel Beresniek, *Symbols of Freemasonry*
6) H. L. Haywood, *Freemasonry and the Bible*
7) John Fellows, *The Mysteries of Freemasonry*
8) A. Holmes-Dallimore, *The Freemason's All In All*
9) J. Walter Hobbs, *Masonic Ritual*
10) Herbert F. Inman, *Masonic Problems and Queries*
11) Herbert Poole, *Masonic Ritual and Secrets Before 1717*
12) Corporation of London, *The Livery Companies of the City of London*
13) W. G. Sibley, *The Story of Freemasonry*
14) H. L. Haywood, *Freemasonry and the Gild System*
15) Douglas Knoop, *Pure Antient Masonry*
16) Douglas Knoop, *The Genesis of Speculative Masonry*
17) Douglas Knoop, *The Mason Word*
18) Kathy Brewis, *Spreading the Word*

An entertaining article on that common practice, the Masonic Fire,
which is carried out after the formal toast

The History of Masonic Firing

(Written in 2004)

Since time immemorial, it has been customary to break bread with one's
friends as a sign of friendship, hospitality and general conviviality. Surely,
there can be no greater honour than for somebody to invite you to sit at their
table and join them, in what these days is often no more than a quick meal,
but that has evolved from a time when man's survival depended on his
hunting prowess, remembering that if he did not catch anything, then he
and his family would have gone hungry.

So by this fact alone the sharing of food is generally one of great
privilege. Likewise, conviviality lead people share drink in a similar vein.

Drink, like food, was also not so easily a gained commodity, as much of
the water could often be contaminated by vegetable debris, insect lava, dead
animals or even dead humans and it therefore became the custom, very early
on in man's existence to make or brew one's own drinks.

For example: Metheglin, a spiced mead and mead in particular, both
made from fermented honey was the earliest of all alcoholic drinks and a
favourite of the Beaker people who inhabited England from about 2000BC.

In fact, in the *Book of the Dead* dated around 4000BC, written in that land between the Euphrates and Tigris, now known as Iraq, where many believe civilization itself first commenced, we find a reference to *"cakes and ale"* which were able to *"perfect souls"*.

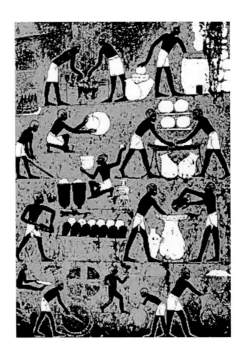

2,000 years later, the mythological *Isis* and her husband *Osiris*, are credited with the introduction of ale to Egypt. It is certain that ale was brewed under the Pharaohs as at that time partly malted barley was baked into a hard loaf, then crumbled, soaked and fermented. The result was an Egyptian drink which according to one source, was called, *boozeh*.

But it was the monks of old that, probably unknown to them, conceived the idea of the tavern, a word derived from Latin meaning hut or booth. Here in the monastery the weary traveller or pilgrim would readily receive a dole of food and drink and a place to rest. These monasteries had well stacked kitchens and flagons of both strong and weak ale. In 1086, the Domesday Book records the Monks of St Paul's Cathedral had brewed some 814 gallons of strong ale. In 1157, we read that Thomas à Becket sent a gift of Canterbury ale to the King of France and there is a record of ale being brewed at Burton Abbey in 1295. However, after the fated dissolution of the monasteries, villagers themselves, began to prepare their own food and brews and sold them on to the traveller.

Those with a little space could offer accommodation, probably with the animals in the stable, and although they would levy a charge, it would at least keep the weary traveller safe from robbers. In due course, we find specially erected buildings built for the sole use of providing safe refuge, rest and refreshment. It was these that slowly became the taverns or inns and places of public resort, where locals and travellers alike could meet. Travellers would bring news from neighbouring counties while the locals would provide services like the blacksmith or ostler who would look after and stable their horses. There, over food and ale, stories, news and tales of the day would be told. Whatever their use, they ultimately became the forerunner of the English public house – that most celebrated and important part of the English way of life which as we known today, is in sad decline.

Old Sign　　　　　　　　　　　　　*New Sign*

As well as strong and weak ale, it also became the custom in taverns such as these to drink, so called health reviving draughts, known as cordials. These home-made cordials or strong waters, as they were known, were believed by the imbiber to have some kind of medicinal quality.

Arnold de Vila Nova, born 1240, an alchemist who lived in Spain wrote of the distillation of wine into *aqua vitae* (Latin for *water of vitality*) and the subsequent flavouring of these spirits with various herbs and spices. In his *Boke of Wine* he wrote of the restorative and life-giving properties of the waters, while Raymond Lully, a student of de Vila Nova believed that so vital were these life restoring waters, they were an inspired gift from Heaven. These cordials were served in measures known as a dram, the term dram probably being taken from the apothecary's measure – *Drachm*. A fluid dram was one eight of a fluid once. These cordials evolved in many ways and were eventually regulated in England under the reign of George III, when an Act of parliament defined them as *"distilled spirituous liquors or strong waters"*. Of course, we know them better as brandy, whisky, rum and gin.

These strong waters were always served in small vessels known either as dram cups or dram glasses, the latter term dating from about 1660. These we were made in flint glass which was considerably stronger than those made with the soda-metal process. They were actually designed to be less liable to suffer breakage in the rough-and-tumble of strong water houses or the Dram-shops as they were known as in the mid-1700s

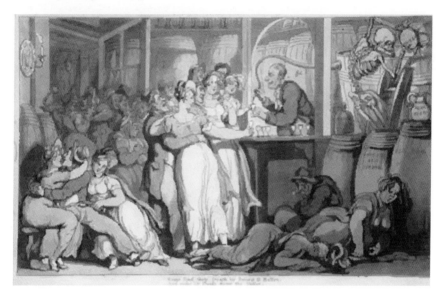

The Dram Shop – by Thomas Rowlandson

The engraving depicts a very real problem that existed in England at that time: the abuse of spirits by the working classes and the poor. Another illustration of this is given in the following poem by William Combe, 1741–1823.

A Preacher, I remember well,
Whose fashion was blunt Truths to tell,
Harangu'd his Audience how to shun
Old Nick, as round the world he run;
And thus the fav'rite haunts defin'd
Of the Great Enemy of Mankind.
"Avoid the place where the profane
"Their Faithless Mysteries maintain;

"Nor let those mansions be explored
"Where the Dice rattles on the board.
"Nor risk your Labour's fair reward
"By shuffling the deceitful Card.
"In haste, pass by the tempting street
"Where the alluring wantons meet;
"For thus, as sure as Evil's evil,
"You'll meet that Spirit call'd the Devil.
"But above all, as you would shun
"In Life and Death to be undone,
"Indulge not in the liquid ill
"That flows from the empoison'd Still,
"Thither the Fiend loves to repair,
"And Death, too oft, attends him there;
"Who, in his never-ceasing rounds,
"The Still-man aids as he compounds
"Each mixture that's in daily strife
"With Health, with Honour, and with Life.
"The Dram-shop is the spot that yields
"More various ills than all the fields
"Where grow the Vices that disgrace
"Th' existence of the human race
"The Town with beggars it supplies,
"And almost fills th' Infirmaries;
"Gives half their inmates to the jails,
"And multiplies the Hangman's vails.
"– Question the sturdy Lab'rer, why
"He wears the rags of Poverty?
"Wherefore his well-paid, daily task
"Denies the Bread his Children ask?

It was during the Georgian period that the practice of rapping glasses upon the table became the common form of acclamation to honour a toast. Hence the glasses used were known as *"thumping"* or *"hammering glasses"*.

The stems of the early firing glasses were short and thick to prevent breakage by such heavy contact, seated on this stem was the bowl which held the liquid.

Now before I progress further with this fascinating subject, I feel I must illuminate the word "Toast". The expression *'to toast'* probably dates back to about the 16th century where traditionally a piece of toasted bread was said to have been put into the loving cup before this was circulated. After each guest had drunk from the cup, the toast was eaten by the host when the cup was returned to him.

This whole process may well have had some form of Christian origin and may well have an allusion to the last supper. The whole idea of sharing wine from a loving cup is often associated with the act of Holy Communion or Eucharist, but that of course is another subject. The correct way of drinking from a loving cup was the man who was drinking had his back guarded by the person on his left while the person on his right guarded his front. It was always felt that a man taking a drink was always at his most vulnerable.

So, we have toasting, a practice which became commonplace and popularised under the reign of the Stuarts, although it was Charles I, that taxed beer for the first time and his son Charles II who made the taxes permanent, thus enhancing the popularity of gin, which remained untaxed.

Hogarth's – Gin Lane

Likewise, I must explain the reason why rapping or thumping glasses were a form of acclamation to honour the toast. Traditionally, it is acknowledged that this custom is representative of the act of firing guns after toasts.

The beginnings of this custom are now lost in the mists of time, but the first record we have of such a practice was recorded by Dr Kuerden in his late 17th century work entitled a *Brief Description of the Burrough and Town of Preston* in which we read the following:

> *"...a Barrel or Hogshead of nappy Ale* (strong ale) *...is broached, and a glass offered to the mayor, who begins a good prosperous health to the King,* (By the way, the term *health* in today's terminology means to toast) *afterwards the Queen, the Nobility and Gentry...at each health begun by Mr Mayor, it is attended with a volley of shott from the musketiers attending...the country people there present drinking the remainder".*

The record goes on to state that the said *"volley of shott"* was repeated *"at the other gate and in the market place".*

The association of the gunfire marked with drinking toasts seems to have been a fairly established custom where guns were available, indicating that it could have a military origin. Thus we read that in 1694, Capt Thomas

Phillips in his account of the voyage of the *Hannibal*", describes how he and Capt Shurley entertained the officers and agents, prior to their departure from Cape Coast Castle on the West African Coast:

> "...having each of us six of our quarter-deck guns brought ashore, with powder &c., and our gunners to ply them; which they did...and made them roar merrily, firing eleven at every health".

The *Dublin News Letter* of June 1741 reported an open-air celebration at Coleraine which was attended by the Mayor and Officers of the Army. Toasts were drunk to the King and the Royal Family:

> "...at each Toast there was a volley from the Army..."

But it was the Bard himself, William Shakespeare, who immortalised this practice in the play Hamlet, written some 400 years ago. When the King proposes and drinks a toast, the stage direction instructs that the toast should be accompanied by a loud report, like that of musket fire.

We can also dispel one theory which relates to the Navy. You may have heard it said on occasion that the glass for which a naval gunner had his daily ration of grog, and the receptacle for which he measured powder into the breach of a cannon were one of the same, hence the name firing-glass. I have researched this theory and can find no evidence of this, although I add that I am not in any way a specialist in these matters, I note that by at least the 1700s, powder was delivered into the cannon in cylindrical packages which were pushed direct into the barrel.

While on the subject of the Navy, I am also reliably informed why toasts taken at Royal Navy Institutions and Lodges are traditionally taken seated. It does not stem from the fact that standing up in a rolling ship can be precarious, but rather the height of the deck where dinner was served. Those participating could neither stand fully erect nor raise their glasses to a full height.

With Masonic records being so sparse, we unfortunately lack any early evidence of customary or traditional ways of toasting although I am happy to confirm that early Freemasons enjoyed greatly the custom of both toasting and drinking.

Andersons *Constitutions* of 1738 tells us that in 1721 when John, Duke of Montague, was elected Grand Master he:

> "...was forthwith saluted Grand Master Elect, and his health drunk in due form..."

In his 1723 edition, Anderson includes several songs which he gives instructions for the toasts, for example it says:

> *"Stop here and drink to the present Grand Master" "Stop her and drink to the health of the Master and Wardens"* and so on.

In the Entered Apprentice song, which we are instructed to sing when all the grave business of the Lodge is over, the first verse ends in:

> *"Here's Health to an Accepted Mason"*

While the last verse concludes:

> *"Then join Hand in Hand*
> *T'each other firm stand*
> *Let's be merry and put a bright face on:*
> *What Mortal can boast*
> *So noble a Toast,*
> *As a Free and Accepted Mason".*

The earliest record of the Masonic fire comes from a French exposure of 1737 which was published by the Lieutenant General of Police with the intention of ridiculing the Craft. It is said that he obtained it from Mademoiselle Carton, a dancer of the Paris Opera, who apparently acquired the information in exchange for her favours.

> *"...after which they sit down and, with the Master's leave, drink the new Brother's Health: every Body has his Bottle. When they have a mind to drink they say, Give some Powder, i.e. fill the Glass.*
>
> *The Master says, Lay your hands to your Firelocks; then they drink the Brother's Health, and the Glass is carried in three different Motions to the Mouth; before they set it down on the Table they lay it to their left breast, then to the right and then forwards, and in three Pauses they lay the Glass perpendicular upon the Table; and clap their Hands three Times!"*

The text, when translated into English seems to lose something and if examined closely does not run like the fire we all know.

Again, we are indebted to the French exposures of the 1740s, from which the following extracts are taken, which gives us greater detail into the actual practice. You will note all the terms used are taken from the artillery.

> *"The bottle was called a barrel, while wine is called red powder and water white powder. The routine which they observe in drinking does not permit the uses of glasses, for there would not be a whole glass left after they had finished. They use goblets which they refer to as Cannon. When they drink in ceremony, the order is given: "Take your powder", at which everybody rises and the Worshipful (Master) says: "Charge". At that point each present fills his goblet. The command then follows: "Present Arms, Take Aim, Fire, Grand Fire". On the first they stretch their hands to the goblet, on the second they raise them as though presenting arms, and on the last they drink.*
>
> *When taking up their goblets they carry them forward a little at first, then to the left breast and across to the right, then in three movements they replace their goblets on the table and clap their hands three times."*

Now if we look closer at our Masonic fire, we can see that there is some repetition of this old French custom.

For example, our current practice is made up of seven triads, that is seven times three, however we must always remember there is absolutely

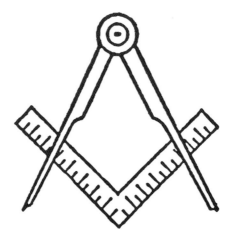

The traditional Square and Compass

no significance, symbolism or hidden meaning in the fire, it is an ancient traditional, convivial and customary practice that was naturally inherited by Freemasonry as something that was practised at the time.

We must also remember that the "Point, Left, Right" does not represent the compasses which are traditionally placed above the Square. Neither is it representative of the Entered Apprentice sign.

It has also been suggested that they are related to the Sign of the Cross for which a brother or minister may wish to make during the offering of Grace.

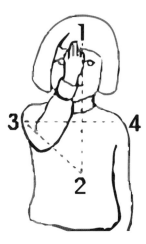

The Sign of the Cross

Another view is that the sign is related to the "Hammer of Thor" sign, which apparently it is indicative of. In ancient times, we read that signs similar to this were made by peoples of the Scandinavian countries in order to placate their great God.

Hammer of Thor

Some believe it is a remnant or vestige of our Operative brothers who most probably used such a motion when spreading cement or mortal with their trowel while in the act of building.

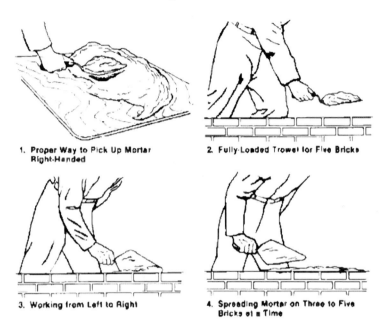

1. Proper Way to Pick Up Mortar Right-Handed

2. Fully-Loaded Trowel for Five Bricks

3. Working from Left to Right

4. Spreading Mortar on Three to Five Bricks at a Time

So, I am guessing the original custom, which as far as I can ascertain, went something like this: The toast was made up of seven triads or 21movements possibly representing the 21 gun salute and remembering that the glass must be drained during each toast.

First three movements are:
1) Point the glass forward, 2) then to the left, 3) then to the right.
Second three movements:
1) Point the glass forward, 2) then to the left, 3) then to the right.
Third three movements:
1) Point the glass forward, 2) then to the left, 3) then to the right.
Fourth three movements:
1) Raise the glass in front of the face slightly above the head, 2) drink the contents of the vessel, 3) bring the vessel down hard on the table.
Fifth three movements:

Three claps.
Sixth three movements:
Three claps.
Seventh three movements:
Three claps.
21 movements in total.

And for those of you that have attended a festive board that uses firing glasses in that way will definitely remember the deafening sound as each glass crashes down on the table.

So far, we have covered several topics relating to both firing and firing glasses and to finish I will make a few observations on the subject of toasts and toasting in general.

For example, how often have we heard a brother proposing a toast with the word "Bumper"? For example, "Brethren, join me in drinking a bumper toast to …" Well, the term "bumper" originally referred to a squat leather cup which, at a later date, came to mean any individual drinking vessel.

There is no connection with the term and the banging of the glasses down on the table, for as we have learnt from an exposure published in France in about 1740, the drinking vessels were referred to as "cannon".

However, in the Masonic setting, the English exposure called *Jachin and Boaz 1762*, the candidate is instructed to "take a bumper" to drink with.

These days when we use the term "bumper", the proposer is merely calling for a hearty response from those present, to the recipient of the toast, which we of course, should all be happy to comply.

It is the same when we are called upon to drink a toast it is always accompanied by the request to be "upstanding".

Now technically this is a slightly absurd request as etiquette demands that all toasts should be taken standing up. As we have heard, it is only the Royal Navy and a few other bodies whose tradition dictates that they take their toasts seated.

The word "upstanding" is not the opposite of "sitting down", it is in fact an obsolete word which in past times made reference to one character and not any specific posture. It is suggested that if that person giving the toast feels the necessity to give that order he should invite the brethren to "Stand and Drink".

JACHIN AND BOAZ;

OR, AN

AUTHENTIC KEY

To the DOOR of

FREE-MASONRY.

Calculated not only for the Inftruction of every New-Made MASON; but alfo for the Information of all who intend to become BRETHREN.

CONTAINING,

I. A circumftantial Account of all the Proceedings in making a Mafon, with the feveral Obligations of an ENTERED APPRENTICE, FELLOW-CRAFT, and MASTER; and alfo the Sign, Grip, and Pafs-Word of each Degree; with the Ceremony of the Mop and Pail.

II. The Manner of opening a Lodge, and fetting the Craft to Work.

III. The *Entered Apprentice, Fellow-Craft,* and *Mafter's Lectures,* verbatim, as delivered in all Lodges; with the Songs at the Conclufion of each Part.

IV. The Origin of Mafonry; Defcription of *Solomon's* Temple; Hiftory of the Murder of the Grand Mafter *Hiram* by the three Fellow Crafts; the Manner of the Affaffins being difcovered, and their Punifhment; the Burial of *Hiram* by King *Solomon's* Order; with the Five Points of Fellowfhip, &c.

V. The Ceremony of the Inftalment of the Mafters of different Lodges on St. *John's* Day.

VI. A fafe and eafy Method propofed, by which a Man may obtain Admittance into any Lodge, without paffing through the Form required, and thereby fave a Guinea or two in his Pocket.

Illuftrated with

An accurate Plan of the DRAWING on the Floor of a Lodge.

And Interfperfed with Variety of

NOTES and REMARKS,

Neceffary to explain and render the Whole clear to the meaneft Capacity.

By a GENTLEMAN belonging to the Jerufalem Lodge; a frequent Vifitor at the Queen's Arms, St. Paul's Church-Yard; the Horn, in Fleet-ftreet; Crown and Anchor, Strand; and the Salutation, Newgate-ftreet.

Try me; prove me.

LONDON:

Printed for W. NICOLL, at the Paper-Mill, St. Paul's Church-Yard.

MDCCLXII.

We also often become confused with the informal wine takings during the meal and the formal toasts after we have eaten. The procedure for informal wine takings taken during the meal when the Master generally takes wine with the following:

- His Wardens, with whom he rules the Lodge
- Grand Lodge Officers or special visitors
- Visiting Masters
- The new Initiate on his first night
- The Officers of the Lodge or those that helped with the ceremony that evening
- Past Masters of and in the Lodge
- Members of the Holy Royal Arch
- The Master's personal guests

These informal wine takings require the recipient to respond by standing and taking wine in the same manner of mutual respect.

THE MASONICAL HARMONY

The formal toasts taken after the meal include:
- The Queen
- The Grand Master
- The Grand Lodge
- The Provincial Grand Master
- The Provincial Grand Lodge

- The Worshipful Master
- The Initiate
- The Guests and Visitors
- The Tylers Toast

In this case the procedure is that each brother stands to join the proposer in wishing health and well-being to the recipient. Etiquette dictates that the recipient of the toast remains seated and does not respond by drinking their own health.

So, to recap, we have learnt how the very act of sharing a drink has always been a great convivial custom. That how drinking each other's health became a great convivial custom and was accompanied with the sound of table rapping or the loud report of canon or musket fire.

We have also learnt how Freemasonry inherited this convivial custom and that the Masonic fire enjoyed at all festive boards is not really a Masonic custom, nor has it any allusion to Freemasonry whatsoever.

We have also learnt the difference between formal and informal toasts and how we seem to have introduced certain words into our toasts which do not have the meaning we actually intended.

But having said all that, as all Lodge customs are different, each tend to follow their own pattern and there must never be any criticism of the manner in which each Lodge, by tradition, conducts its Festive board, and my words are neither compulsory nor advisory, but merely the informative findings of my research on a given subject.

Therefore brethren, although you have heard some different suggestions, manners or procedures on the subject of toasting and firing, you will of course totally ignore these and as ever observe your own Lodge customs and traditions and continue to "take your time" and instruction from your ever-present Director of Ceremonies.

The Church and the Cathedral Builders

(Written in 2003)

My lecture to night is to establish the link or show the influence that the Cathedral Builders and the Church have had on Freemasonry and it will be well to remember that specific objective as this lecture tends to cover several subjects very quickly.

After recently reading two books entitled *How To Read A Church* by Richard Taylor and *Guided By A Stone-Mason* by Thomas Maude, I became absolutely fascinated by the symbols and terminology used by the medieval stone mason, the Church and how these knowingly or unknowingly have been incorporated into Freemasonry. I must state from the onset of this lecture that I have never particularly subscribed to that commonly argued theory of the Transition, which basically claims that Operative Freemasonry over a period of time, and starting in England, slowly became an organisation of Non-Operative or Gentlemen Masons. However, having studied this subject in some depth, I can only say that my long-held view of the development of our Fraternity is currently under review and as I share my findings, you may well review your own opinions.

We know that the men of the medieval builder's trade were artisans, highly skilled and educated and it is not an understatement to say that they were the ablest of men the Middle Ages produced. They designed and constructed hundreds of cathedrals, chapels, monasteries, castles and fortresses, many were illiterate, but their apprenticeship in this art, which at the time was considered the greatest of all and was so thorough, that as a group of men they possessed among themselves so large a body of knowledge, that a Master of this trade was considered more educated than a Bishop.

The principles of the Gothic cathedral, in which the almost impossible task of raising a perpendicular using weight, counter balance, pinnacles and flying buttresses, were their discovery. Their art, which was their monopoly, enabled them to produce a building which was unequalled in the past by no other architecture except the Greek, and has yet to be surpassed. Yet it was the Church that seemed to hold this body of men together and stimulate that most fascinating period of man's building ability.

Logically, the church, and in particular the Abbots and Bishops held so much power and knowledge during that period, that it is fair to say they possibly controlled it. In fact, one school of thought has been that the Church actually formed the Trade Fraternities. It is a fact that each trade group, Masons being no exception to this, had Patron Saints, built niches and lit candles to worship them, held feast days to celebrate them, funded a Priest to offer them pastoral care, often paying for the upkeep of a Chapel and even participating in the miracle plays which goes to show that they had more than just a passing association with them.

History shows us that the Church and the Masons were never that far apart, and from the Masons view, they were building these great edifices to God and in turn the Church funded the great religious buildings and provided employment. It is therefore no wonder then that we find in the earliest of operative records, and I refer to the Regius and Cooke MS, references to the development of the builder's craft from the earliest of times, although they do not contain specific details about the Temple of King Solomon, as one might imagine, for this was to be an 18th century innovation into Masonic fable.

It does include however, details of the Sons of Lamech who discovered the Arts and Sciences, specifically geometry, the building of the Tower of Babylon, the story of Nimrod and the City of Nineveh and the education of the "sons" of the Egyptians, in the ways of Masonry by Euclid, all neatly sown together so as to form the mystical legend of the Craft. In the Regius MS, we may also read the legend of the Four Crowned or Martyred Ones, who were 3rd century Christian sculptures that were put to death for refusing to carve a statue of Aesculapius for the Emperor Diocletian. The acts of these martyrs were preserved for history by a revenue officer named Porphyrius, probably in the 4th century.

Also found in these old MS and many later ones are the moral rules and codes of behaviour for these operatives. Known to us collectively as the "Old Charges", they were placed in our first *Book of Constitutions* in 1723, and although still to be found there, these days they are seldom used or referred to. So, the basis of our science, i.e. the moral rules and codes of conduct were taken from these 14th century documents which as we now know were possible copies from an even earlier document, as the Cooke MS seems to indicate. The Polycronicon was written in Latin by Ranulph Higden probably about a century earlier; therefore, we could concede that our legendary history appears to start much earlier than general considered opinion.

Let us now take look at some of the things we see at every meeting and are familiar with us, those tangible elements of our Craft which allude to that association we have with the Cathedral builders. Our starting place will be here in the Lodge room, which we all know is representative of an operative's workshop.

Beetles, Mauls and Gavels

Yes! They are known by different names but I will not speak about that in this lecture. The maul you will understand is the driving implement that moves the chisel whereas the gavel is a derived from the stonecutter's axe which was used in an entirely different way from the maul, i.e. to roughly shape blocks rather than carve detail.

The Chisel

This implement comes in many different shapes, and was said to be one of the main influences in the development of the detailed and ornamental Gothic architecture style. For Masonic use, it is always depicted in its simplest form i.e. that which is used for smoothing, but each different chisel, when employed by the artisan, can produce the most intricate of carvings.

The Twenty-Four Inch Gauge

This imperial standard was a simply measuring device and would have been used in many trades.

The Square, the Level and the Plumb Rule

These are three of the most basic tools again used by many trade to ensure accuracy.

The Skirret

A simple but effective device for marking out ground in preparation for the foundations of a building.

The Pencil and the Compasses
Used for marking, designing, planning, measuring and illustrating.

The Tripod and Lewis
The Tripod or Derrick, is a supporting device to which a simple pulley is attached, whereas the Lewis is a device used to lift stones which slots into a dovetailed opening and expands when lifted and contracts for removal when released.

The Tracing Boards
Standard equipment used for plans in the preparation and illustration of diagrammatical information, again the starting point for most projects.

The Ashlars
These are the apprentice's first active work and give actual illustration of roughhewn and polished stone. Used in the construction of basic square-stone buildings and probably used as a standard measurement depending on the requirements of each building.

Aprons
Standard safety equipment to keep clothing clean and protect the worker from the sharp edges of the stone.

Gloves and Gauntlets
Again, both used for the protection of the worker.

All these items mentioned are found in our Lodge rooms and can be seen at every meeting, but it is not only the tools and garb of the workman that are found here which possible identify us with or that provide an operative link, you will also find the **Warrant or Charter**, which was formerly required by law, by all trades to regulate and control quality and to give authority to exist, to operate or to build.

The Book of Constitutions or regulations were another requirement by law which had to be presented as part of the application of the Charter and which explained the aims and objectives or purpose for the application.

Therefore, as you can see, attendance at any regular Lodge meeting will immediately reveal our heritage, but it does not stop there for in other Orders we find further evidence of this Operative connection. For example, in the Holy Royal Arch we are introduced to the **Pick, the Crow, and the Shovel**, all used in the excavation process for the foundations of the building. **Ropes**, employed in the movement of heavy blocks and to secure the safety of any man working at a height. **The trowel**, a tool still used today to spread the mortar or cement between stones or bricks.

While in the Mark Degree, like the Operative of old, each brother is distinguished by a **Mark**. This mark was ascribed to all of his work to ensure quality and payment for work produced. There are also **Diagrams** which are used like a template to prove the shape of a stone is true. **T-squares and Set squares,** used to test accuracy.

In fact, if we look back in time at the trade associations, the Company of Masons, which was set up some four centuries before Grand Lodge employed Officers in the capacity of **Masters, Wardens, Secretary, Treasurer and Almoner**. And who would ever dispute the terms **Entered Apprentice** (the names of those entered on the company roll) and **Fellow Craft** (that fellow of the Craft who had accomplished his apprenticeship) were not directly attributed to that Company of Operatives? Even more so like those medieval trade associations and in the early days of Craft Masonry, before its de-Christianisation, we even had two **Patron Saints**, St John the Baptist and St John the Evangelist, whose feast days were likewise celebrated.

Little doubt then that our Lodge rooms were ever intended to replicate or represent an operative's workshop for these were the places where the business of the day was conducted. These included instructions, appointments and discipline much like we use them today. Workers of other trades, or labourers were not allowed into these Lodge rooms or site huts, although I can find no evidence to suggest that they were tiled in any way, other than the general warnings regarding eavesdroppers.

To examine this relationship a little closer, I began a study of the erection of the Gothic Cathedral and I soon discovered a little more information. This however started to crossover with the practices of the Church and soon I realised how close the two were intertwined. We can of course makes no real allusions to the fact that our terminology appears to replicate that of the Church and its Builders, but things have to start somewhere and links, however tenuous they may seem, become chains as another thread is added to them.

The Mosaic Floor

Legend has it that the floor of the Tabernacle in the wilderness was chequered, and that the floor of Solomon's Temple was also chequered, in imitation of the Tabernacle. Unfortunately, I have not been able to source this legend and it does not seem to be of Biblical origin. However, a colleague suggested that it was an old Hebrew legend possibly from the writings of Josephus. Whatever its origin, the fact remains that many religious buildings, Westminster Abbey being the obvious, has a black and white chequered floor, albeit in that particular case, running diagonally rather than square.

The term Regular

If the Cathedral was deemed "regular," it was part of a monastery. The clergy were the monks who lived and conducted their lives by strict monastic rule of whichever the Order they were part of. They took little notice of what was happening in the outside world and kept themselves entirety to themselves. History shows us that in many cases when Masons arrived ready for work, houses were sometimes built for them and they tended to keep themselves in tight little communities and were probably looked upon by the locals as suspicious strangers. In today's Craft, our work and business is kept strictly within the realms of our "regular" Lodges.

The term Chapter

I was fascinated to learn that each cathedral was ran by a group of clergy called a "Chapter".

Three, Five and Seven

Very significant to our Craft as you recall, three rule a Lodge, five hold a Lodge, and seven make a Lodge perfect. It was with surprise that I noted that the development of those high pointed or lancet windows, were generally built in threes, fives, or sevens.

The religious significance of these numbers are as follows: **Three,** represents God the Father, God the Son and God The Holy Ghost. It can also represent the three days Jesus spent in the tomb prior to his resurrection. Incidentally three was also the number who watched over the cathedral business, the Dean and his two assistants. **Five**, represents the five wounds Jesus received while on the cross, two in his hands, two in his feet and one in his side. **Seven**, which appears repeatedly throughout the bible and represents perfection. Examples are: God rested on the seventh day after the creation. (Genesis 2:1-3). God ordered the lamp stand for the Tabernacle should have seven branches. (Exodus 25:37). The seven Angels blowing their trumpets in the apocalypse. (Revelations 8-11).

The East

Facing the East probably predates any Christian significance and of course facing the Sun rise during worship is a universal custom. The Gothic cathedral or the early churches however, were built in the same fashion, and their position depended to whom or to which Saint the building was to be dedicated. Wherever the Sun rose and set on that Saints day, so the building would run from East to West. The Bishop always sat in the East and it was said that the worshipers would face East, or that point where Jesus was Crucified. As you know, our Lodges also lie on that East to West axis with the Master always seated in the East.

Volume of Sacred Law

We understand how important the Bible, is to Freemasonry, so much so that the Chaplain's jewel, if you look close enough, has the words Holy Bible written on an open book of Scripture, surmounted by a glory.

In the Operative setting, the earliest reference I can find for the use of the Bible in Oath taking is found in the *Grand Lodge No 1 MS*, dated 1583, and roughly translated says:

> *"...then one of the elders holds out a book and he or they shall place their hands upon it and the following precepts shall be read."*

Obviously, there is no indication if the book which ones hand was placed upon was a Bible, but we know that by this date copies of the Bible were in circulation, albeit only the four gospels, but it would be fair to say not that many. Suggestions have been made that the word "book" refers to a *Book of Constitutions* or a *Book of Charges*. However, I do not necessarily subscribe to this theory on the basis that one would not take an Oath on pain of death, on a *book of charges as it would not hold the significance of a Bible nor would it strike fear* in one's heart like a Bible would. Secondly, that although Bibles were few in number, if there was this connection with the Church and the guilds as previously covered, then in all probability it would have been a Bible.

I think it a reasonable assumption that 23 years later it was a Bible that was used in 1606, by the Barbers and Surgeons Guild whose records say:

"You shall concale, keep secrett and not disclose such councill as att any tyme hereafter shall be used or spoken of by or amongst the said company soe help me God and by the Holy contents of this Booke."

Evidence also that it was not only Masons that had secrecy bound by oaths.

Let me talk for a minute or two in general terms about some of the other aspects that touch on Builder, Church and Freemason alike.

The colour Blue

That beautiful sky-blue that adorns our aprons, was in the medieval church, and still today, the colour that is associated with the Virgin Mary and Jesus. In Numbers 15:37-40 we can read why we have this fringe of colour?

37. And the Lord spake unto Moses saying,
38. Speak unto the children of Israel, and bid them that they make them fringes in the borders of their garments throughout their generations, and that they put upon the fringe of the borders a ribbon of blue:
39. And it shall be unto you for a fringe, that ye may look upon it, and remember all the commandments of the Lord,
40. That ye may remember, and do all my commandments, and be holy unto your God.

It is, as the scripture says, to remind us of all the commandments of the Lord.

The Square

In the form of a cube, it is a symbol of the earth, and used as a halo on images of holy people who were still alive at the time when the image was made.

The Triangle

Is a symbol of the Trinity, equilateral in nature representing the equality of the three persons of the Godhead.

The Circle

Thus considered to be the perfect shape of eternity, no beginning and no end and seen by the church as being divine.

The Qualifications of its Members

Let us now look at the qualifications of its Members which, like the Operative masons of old, Speculative masonry has also always required certain qualifications of its Apprentices.

The *Old MS Charges* for example, required an apprentice to be of honest parents, probably a result of priestly influence, (we have already established the role of the church with the early guilds) and almost certainly based upon the early Christian practice of not allowing bastards to enter the priesthood. This observance obviously being taken literally by the readers of Deuteronomy 23:2 which reads:

> "*A bastard shall not enter into the congregation of the Lord; even to their tenth generation shall he not enter into the congregation of the Lord.*"

Bastards were generally considered unfit people and again we can read in Zechariah 9:6 how they were penalised:

> "*A bastard shall not dwell in the city of Ashdod.*"

In his book, *Freemasons Guide and Compendium*, Bernard E. Jones tells us that:

> "*The Old Charges of a Freemason accompanying the Constitutions of the United Grand Lodge state that "no master should take an apprentice unless…he should be descended of honest parents," and we know that in the superstitious days of the 1700s many speculative lodges took this old direction quite literally, believing that the illegitimate child was spiritually unfit…*"

It was a similar situation regarding one's physical attributes, certainly one would need to be in good physical condition if engaged in a heavy trade like construction yet why would this stipulation be brought into Speculative masonry? In 1809, minutes from the Maid's Head Lodge at Norwich ceased the ceremony of Initiation on the grounds that:

"...in consequence of his not being upright in body, he could not be admitted..."

Again, we can cite such scriptures as Leviticus 21:18-21:

18. For whatsoever man he be that have a blemish, he shall not approach: a blind man, or a lame, or he that hath a flat nose, or any thing superfluous,
19. Or a man that is broken footed or broken handed,
20. Or crookback, or a dwarf, or that have a blemish in his eye, or be scurvy, or scabbed, or hath his stones broken;
21. No man that hath a blemish of the seed of Aaron the priest shall come nigh to offer the offerings of the Lord made by fire; he hath a blemish; he shall not come nigh to offer the bread of his God.

Fortunately, we can categorically state today that neither of these two qualifications needs to be met in their literal sense. To bar a prospective member on these grounds would be an act of discriminations and a great injustice to the whole ethos of the Craft for which the only real qualification is one of age, belief and good character.

Talking of one's character, as the Candidate stands at the door of the Lodge in a state of darkness, humbly soliciting to be admitted into masonry, the Master has an exchange of words with the Inner Guard culminating in the affirmation that the candidate is of good report. This phrase "of good report" can be found in Philippians 4:8 where it says:

"Finally, brethren, whatsoever things are true, whatsoever things are honest, whatsoever things are just, whatsoever things are pure, whatsoever things are lovely, whatsoever things are of good report..."

I found the phrase used in seven other scriptures of both the Old and New Testament.

The Three Candles
The candles that burn at the pedestals of the Master and his two Wardens

again have an allusion to three specific areas. In early Lodges in England and still in many overseas Lodges, the candles form parts of a triangular alter that is found in the center of the Lodge room. Apart from representing Wisdom (WM), Strength (SW) and Beauty (JW), they are supported by three candlesticks designed in three specific styles of architectural column, namely Ionic (WM), Doric (SW), and Corinthian (JW). In the Church, candles can represent a number of things including, light of life, hope, a message that illuminates the world and even the passing of goodness and brotherly love from one to another, all relevant to the ethos of Freemasonry.

Hope

The symbol of hope, often seen on the First Degree and the Mark Tracing Board as an Anchor or better described as the Anchor Cross. The Cross itself, was not a symbol of the early Christians, they actually used the anchor which like the fish was probably used as a secret sign. In Christian terms, the anchor is specifically a symbol of hope of salvation and eternal life. The message clearly woven into the trigradal system we practice today, although not from an overtly Christian sense, but if you look closely, you will still find several Christians allusions.

There is little doubt that the Operative Craft was Catholic in its orientation. Not that it could have been anything else from the point that it was formed before the reformation when the church in general was directed form Rome. It is therefore wrong of us to say that early Speculative Freemasonry did not carry a Christian or pre-reformation message. I will demonstrate that now.

The first point is from that most instructive Degree, the Third or Master Masons Degree, which teaches us how to die, coupled with the hope of eternal salvation. Masonic scholars in general have little doubt that the main message of this degree is the symbolic resurrection of the faithful to eternal life. Just to remind us, I will read those words used by the Worshipful Master who having just raised the Candidate from his would-be tomb when he delivers to him this Charge:

> *"...that the Lord of Life will enable us to trample the King of Terrors beneath our feet, and lift our eyes to that bright Morning Star, whose rising brings peace and salvation to the faithful and obedient..."*

Many have believed that this bright morning star is Venus, rising just shortly before the Sun. Why? I do not know because the planet Venus has never had such a promise attached to it. Yet if we read Revelations 22:11, we are left in no doubt:

> *"I Jesus have sent mine angels to testify unto you these things*
> *in the churches. I am the root and the offspring of David, and*
> *the bright and morning star."*

Further evidence to this allusion can be found in the Lodges of our devout Jewish brethren who, not acknowledging Jesus as the Messiah and being embarrassed by this message, have changed those third-degree words to the following:

> *"...and lift our eyes to Him (Him meaning God) whose divine*
> *Word brings Peace and Salvation to the faithful..."*

This slight alteration proved both acceptable to brethren of all faiths and more suitable to the religious stance of the Craft.

While in the same degree there is another allusion when the candidate is asked to place his feet in a certain position while experiencing the drama. That it is while his feet are in this position he is made to represent Jesus on the cross for there are grounds to believe that this was the position of his feet during the Crucifixion. An allusion which is certainly new to me, but considered by some to have a Christian significance. I can see it could possibly have some credence on the basis that the candidate is placed in this position immediately the wardens take the place of those ruffians and prior to his symbolic demise as if to demonstrate humiliation.

What is a clearer allusion is the position the new Initiate is placed in after he has been invested with that distinguishing badge of a Mason, the North East part of the building, where he then figuratively represents the foundation or corner stone. Ephesians 2:20-21, tells us that:

> *"...Jesus Christ himself being the chef corner stone...In whom*
> *the building fitly framed together growth unto an holy temple*
> *in the Lord."*

It was James Anderson, one of those founding fathers of Grand Lodge, who stands accused of starting the de-Christianising of the Craft, it being finished by the Duke of Sussex almost a century later. However, that the Craft was ever in need of this process is a matter of opinion and I consider that it has never really been hotly debated, but no sooner did this process start then so-called Christian degrees began to spring up, mainly on the continent, but soon arriving in England. These degrees, which satisfied the religious appetite of the Christian Freemason, have become very popular today. Although not technically endorsed by Grand Lodge or the General Laws and Regulations for the Government of the Craft, the fact remains that most Grand Lodge Officers belong to them which is a paradox in itself and a contradiction as men join an organisation free from religious dogma and then join a deeply religious Degree. They then lose that basic principle of the Craft whereby they previously were able to rub shoulders and work in perfect harmony with Jew, Muslim and Hindu alike, finding that perfect medium of conciliating friendship amongst those who would otherwise have remained at a perpetual distance. However, as Jew, Muslim and Hindu alike, do not qualify to join these Degrees I believe it is demeaning.

It is at that point of their progression in their Masonic career that they then degrade that stance by joining another organisation, under the same banner, which precludes those very brethren because of their beliefs. A fact which I find not only distasteful but a practice alien to the Great Landmarks of the Craft.

I must add at this point that this is a personal belief not intended to offend any of my good friends and colleagues who are associated with these degrees, nor am I intending to cheapen or debase any Christian degrees, however for the Craft to find the beliefs of Christianity so distasteful is also displeasing, and those reviewers of our ritual failed miserable in completing their task as the ritual abounds with Christian allusions.

Likewise, if Christianity was found to be so repugnant, Judaism was not, for the stories revolve completely around the Old Testament. Had the legend of the Craft dealt exclusively with the building of King Solomon's Temple, purely as the first House to be constructed to the Glory of God by Masons, then this could be readily accepted and the fact is, there were many other facets added to the story to make it more attractive and in an endeavour to forsake one creed, I consider that they have almost embraced another. The Craft always had to have some religious allusion and since Anderson felt it compulsory to initially embrace the Operative Charges and practices then the inclusion of pre-reformation religious instances were inevitable.

In my own mind, there is now absolute concrete evidence to demonstrate that Freemasonry has inherited, adopted, stolen or copied its usages, practices and observances from other or earlier organisations. The Lodge room itself, contains all the implements, although ornamental, of a workshop. The reason they are ornamental is that we are speculative and not operative Freemasons and the working tools and implements of that trade are there for us to moralise upon and act as visual reminders or symbols for our ultimate aim which is to raise a superstructure, perfect in its parts (our thoughts, words and deeds) and honourable to the builder (The Great Architect), Freemasonry helping us to lay the foundation for that structure. And that is the sole aim of Freemasonry, personal improvement.

This evening we have examined the links between the Church, the Cathedral Builders and Freemasonry, however, how, where or why the development took place from Operative to Speculative we do not know, but we do have documentary evidence by way of Lodge records and minutes, of Operative and Non-Operative Masons working together in Scotland and Operative and Accepted Masons in England. Ultimately, we also know that it was the Non-Operative, Accepted or Speculative Freemason that went on to develop Freemasonry to what it is today.

An examination of the demands placed upon each member of the Craft including a history and commentary on the Charge to the Initiate

Exactly what does Freemasonry Demand of Us?

(Written in 2004)

The very first step we take under the auspices of Freemasonry is our interview with the Lodge committee, which as you may recall is generally made up of the Master, his Wardens and the Past Masters of and in the Lodge.

It is here, while not even under oath, but of our own free will and accord, we make that single most important declaration upon which is based our entrance into the Craft and the start of our masonic journey. If answered incorrectly it will impede our entry into this noble science. That simple question upon which rests the whole of the Craft and demands the affirmative in its answer is, "Do you believe in a God?"

DO YOU

BELIEVE

?

Often couched more eloquently in terms of reference, Supreme Being for example or the Great Architect of the Universe, probably being the most common examples, it is demanded of us, before witnesses, to reveal that most personal of all our relationships: That which we have with our Deity. It must occur to many at that time that such a personal solicitation must indicate that one is about to seek admission into some great religious foundation, but of course we are wrong. Freemasonry is not a religion, but it does require all its adherents to be religious.

From the Quarterly Communications of the United Grand Lodge of 9 December 1981 we read the following:

> *"It cannot be too strongly asserted that masonry is neither a religion nor a substitute for religion. Masonry seeks to inculcate in its members a standard of conduct and behaviour which it believes to be acceptable to all creeds, but studiously refrains from intervening in the field of dogma or theology. Masonry therefore, is not a competitor with religion though in the sphere of human conduct it may be hoped that its teachings will be complimentary to that of religion. On the other hand its basic requirement that every member of the Order shall believe in a Supreme Being and the stress laid upon his duty towards Him should be sufficient evidence to all but the wilfully prejudiced that masonry is an upholder of religion since it both requires a man to have some form of religious*

belief before he can be admitted as a Mason, and expects him when admitted to go on practising his religion."[1]

Grand Lodge explains quite clearly that stress be laid upon our duty toward God and that we are expected, once admitted, to go on practising our religion.

Although not a religion in itself, the Craft is built upon the purist values of piety and virtue and founded upon the Grand Principles of Brotherly Love, Relief and Truth.

Let us therefore be reminded exactly what we agreed, accepted and acknowledged previously to taking our Obligation as an Initiate:

1 Prior to our Initiation, we declared to the Lodge committee, without equivocation and by our own volition, our belief in a Supreme Being.

2 As we paid our dues to the Treasurer, we read and signed our name in the declaration book which stated that we:

> *"...cheerfully conform to all the antient usages and the established customs of the Order."* As per Rule 162, *Book of Constitutions*, United Grand Lodge of England.

3 At the start of the ceremony we declared in open Lodge, that in times of difficulty and danger we place our trust in God.[2]

4 Likewise, we answered three questions again in open Lodge prior to taking our Obligation which included the following statements; a) *"...we freely and voluntary offer ourselves as a candidate..."* b) *"...we have a sincere wish to render ourselves more extensively serviceable to our fellow-creatures..."* c) *"...after our Initiation we will act and abide by the ancient usages and established customs of the Order."* [3]

5 We affirmed our willingness to proceed with the ceremony by accepting the invitation to take a vow of fidelity that would not be incompatible with our religious duties.[4]

Therefore, in reaching this stage, we have freely and cheerfully chosen to accept the many facets of Freemasonry, including its codes of conduct, its customs and its practices.

Of course, tests, trials or qualifications are by no means alien to fraternity membership and since the dawn of time, men have sought to associate themselves with one another for numerous reasons. However, it is not so much the demands of qualificational requirement that needs our attention, but the rules, regulations and bye-laws that go to make up the society. Freemasonry being no exception, expects, or should I say demands standards in three areas of our lives – Brotherly or Fraternally, Ethically, and Morally, and we have cheerfully agreed to accept those demands placed upon us on all those occasions prior to our Obligation when we freely gave our affirmation while under strict observance. In essence, we knew before we fully committed ourselves that such demands and expectations would be placed upon us and freely agreed to be placed under such an obligation.

That great evening of our Initiation passes off so quickly that we generally fail to absorb many of these points within our sub-conscious. However, Freemasonry is kind to us; she lets us undergo the ceremony of Initiation on numerous other occasions throughout our Masonic career. First, as the Initiate, second, as a guide when acting in the office of Junior

Deacon, third, from the Chair of King Solomon as the instructor and of course on all other occasions as an observer or other office holder.

The rite, as we all quickly realise, does not end with the Obligation and subsequently we are given signs, words and tokens, as well as tests, trials, and further instruction, the whole ceremony itself culminates in that wonderful address which must stand alone as the epitome of Masonic conduct and behaviour, The Charge. Based upon the working documents of the Operative Masons, the Charge was rehearsed to all members admitted to the fraternity, be they working Operatives, Accepted or Speculative Masons.

It is in effect a precise guide to the duties and expectations of each and every member and sections have stood the test of time. In parts, dating from that earliest Masonic document, *The Regius Poem*, c.1390, and earlier still from the pen of Mencius, (see note A) c.370 BC, a contemporary of Confucius. In his book, now classed as a Chinese Classic he wrote:

> *"A man should abstain from doing unto others what he would not they should do to him...This is called the principle of acting on the square."*[5]

Therefore, it is not an exaggeration when we are told in the opening sentence that our institution is ancient.

"Every duty is a charge, but the charge of oneself is the root of all others."

Mencius

As a brief history lesson upon which our present-day *Charge* was based, the charges as they were referred to in the *Old Manuscripts*, (see note B) vary in both number and arrangement. There are, for example, 15 Articles for the Master and 15 Points for the Craftsman found in *The Regius Poem*, while the *Cooke* MS, *c*.1450, sets out 9. *The Grand Lodge* MS, *c*.1583, gives 9 general and 18 special charges, both addressed to the Masters and Fellows. There are as one might imagine, a great many other variations. *The Harleian* MS *No 1942, c*.1670, along with a few others that form the Robert's family group of MS sets forth 25 charges and adds six new articles, not found in any prior specimen and introduces the addition of charges for the Apprentice.

It was from these aged documents that Dr Anderson wrote the first Constitutions in 1723. Having said that, we learn from the pen of E. R. Whitfield, in his work, *The Evolution of the Second and Third Degrees*,[6] that Dr Anderson found that between June 1719 and June 1720 several valuable manuscripts concerning the ancient *"regulations, charges, secrets and usages"* were *"burnt by some scrupulous brethren, that those papers might not fall into strange hands."*

Wallace McLeod sums up the situation well in his lecture entitled *The Old Charges*,[7]

> *"In the second edition of his Constitutions, printed in 1738.....He reports that at the Annual Festival on 24 June 1720, when Grand Lodge was one year old, the new Grand Master, George Payne, 'desired any Brethren to bring to the Grand Lodge any old Writings and Records concerning Masons and Masonry in order to shew the Usages of antient Times; And this Year several old copies of the Gothic Constitutions were produced and collated."*

Even in those early days there were reticent Masons who did not choose to risk disclosure. In his narrative of 1720, Anderson says, *"This year, at some private Lodges, several very valuable Manuscripts...concerning the fraternity, their lodges, regulations, Charges, secrets, and Usages...were burnt."* The next year, at the Quarterly Communications of 29 September 1721, the Grand Master, His Grace the Duke of Montagu, and the Grand Lodge, *"finding Fault with all the Copies of the old Gothic Constitutions, order'd Brother James Anderson, A.M., to digest the same in a new and better Method."* This collation of documents was the start of some of the ritual and practices that have culminated in today's ceremonies.

Whilst on this subject, I have heard claims that so much was lost by the action of those so-called "scrupulous brethren" that the true secrets of masonry are no longer to be found. To the exponents of this theory I must point out that most historians concede that that which was destroyed was probably no more than copies of the Old Operative Charges. Although valuable to the Fraternity, it is doubtful that they would have contained any more information than that which already existed in the old MS form that escaped such treatment, or that were later to be revealed by the 18th century exposures.

The next record of the Charge we find is dated 1735, and according to the work of that great Masonic Scholar Harry Carr, *The Freemason at Work*,[8] is the earliest known Speculative version. Anonymously written, it was first published in *Smith's Pocket Companion* (see note C) and in places its language and theme still shines through in today's version. William Preston in his *Illustrations of Masonry*, (see note D) continued to hone the *Charge* through his nine editions which spanned 40 years, 1772–1812. With various slight modifications during the 19th century, the *Charge* which is given today under the many jurisdictions throughout the world differs only in wording, not sentiment, and each of us will recall, although probably having heard it so many times, that it still remains fresh, vibrant and inspiring.

I would like at this point to examine this small piece of ritual a little closer. For the sake of regularity and as Emulation is so widely popular in this area, I will use that version. You will recall its starts with those immortal words;

> *"...let me congratulate you on being admitted a member of our ancient and honourable institution."*[9]

We have already heard how one part of the charge is similar to a document which is over two thousand years old and other parts from another over 600 years old, so the debate as to whether our institution is actually ancient is confirmed. We must also remember that, except for the Royal Society, Freemasonry is the oldest society in England, so we must concede that it is in fact ancient. Of course, we can always argue that although the Royal Society pre-dates the official formation Masonry by 57 years, our masonic documents pre-date the Royal Society by almost three centuries.

> *"...honourable it must be acknowledged...as by a natural tendency it conduces to make those so who are obedient to its precepts."*[10]

Would you say that attending our Lodge meetings, our rehearsals, our ladies nights or some other masonic function makes us honourable? No! It is following the precepts of Masonry that make us honourable, precepts being its laws and its principles. Those students of the V. of S.L. will recall those words: *"Ye shall know them by their fruits."* Matt 7:16, *King James Version*. Honourable men will be recognised by the precepts they practice. Freemasonry advocates *"the practice of every moral and social virtue"*[11] and all the time we practice those virtues, the world will see us as honourable.

> *"...so high an eminence has its credit been advanced that in every age monarchs themselves have been promoters of the art..."[12]*

This is so true, for we have seen how, as the knowledge of our speculative art was carried throughout Europe and the known world, Kings, Princes and Potentates subsequently became Grand Masters or patrons of Freemasonry in their respective countries.

> *"...have not thought it derogatory to their dignity to exchange the sceptre for the trowel..."[13]*

This phrase has great significance, for although the trowel, as a working tool, has long since lost its symbolic significance and has disappeared from most workings in the Craft throughout England, it still holds a place in the Holy Royal Arch. In which ceremony, along with the sword, reminds us of those who built the second temple at Jerusalem, and who were ready to defend themselves as they laid the stones.[14]

On a historical note, in England, the use of the trowel seems to have lost its place at about the time of the Union, 1813. According to H. F. Inman:[15] *"...early Speculative Masons called the trowel the "Emblem of Circumspection" or the "Jewel of the Entered Apprentice" who were exhorted to "stop up all interstices in the lodge so that not a sound shall escape." The Junior Entered Apprentice, it may be noted, at one time discharged the duties similar to those now entrusted to the Inner Guard for whom the earliest known reference of appointment was December 1814."*

In Bristol, it is still used as a working tool of the Master Mason and in America it is well known to signify the spreading of the cement of brotherly love. In recent times, it use has been restored as the jewel of office of the Charity Steward.

The next section of the Charge deals with our relationship with our Creator. Although I must stress at this point that although such a relationship is both private and personal to the individual, I shall make just a few general observations.

> *"...that great, though emblematical light in Freemasonry... the V. of S.L."*

In giving proofs of our proficiency in the first degree, we learn very quickly the answer to the Masters question, "Where were you made a Mason?" Our immediate response is, "In the body of a Lodge, just, perfect and regular." A Lodge cannot fulfil those three conditions without the V of S.L. being open on the Master's pedestal. This is classed as the Lodge being *"just"* and this being one of the Landmarks of the Order, it is the solemn and universal practice of all Lodges constituted under the jurisdiction of the United Grand Lodge of England. It does not have to be a bible, as in general terms, the ethos of all of the world's religions have one thing in common, namely the recognition of a Supreme Being. This as we have previous discussed is deemed a sufficient requirement for the Craft.

It is sad to say that this was the reason that in 1878, the United Grand Lodge of England withdrew its recognition from the Grand Orient of France. They were guilty of transgressing two of the Great Landmarks of the Order. They excluded from its ceremonies the name of the Great Architect of the Universe and the V of S.L. from its L:odges.[16]

The Charge then goes on to explain that the V of S.L. teaches us:

"...the important duties you owe to God, to your neighbour and to yourself."[17]

Masonry exhorts us never to mention the name of our God but with awe and reverence. The Israelitish people, you may recall, never mentioned His name and the true pronunciation was lost. They substituted one of the other names of God, usually Adonai. This points me to those words repeated by the Principal Sojourner when asked by the Most Excellent Zerubbabel to reveal the discovery of great importance found on the plate of gold:

"That Most Excellent, we must humbly beg to decline, for we have heard with our ears, and our fathers have declared unto us, that in their days and the old time before them it was not lawful for anyone to pronounce the name of the True and Living God Most High, save the High Priest, nor him but once a year, when he entered the Holy of Holies and stood before the Ark of the Covenant to make propitiations for the sins of the people."[18]

We are also taught to implore his aid "in all our lawful undertakings and every emergency." This again you may recall we had already affirmed to the Master, as we knelt in darkness, after the Chaplain uttered that prayer of supplication asking for the Supreme Governor of the Universe to endue us with competency.

Our relationship with our neighbour, you may remember, is called;

"...acting with him on the square..."

and we are instructed to offer him;

"...every kind office which justice and mercy may require."

This means we must show kindness, compassion, tolerance, magnanimity and patience.

"And to ourselves..."

says the Charge, by;

"...walking uprightly before God...and steering the bark of this life over the seas of passion without quitting the helm..."

so we can;

"...exert those talents wherewith God has blessed us with for His glory and the welfare of our fellow creatures."

At the front of the *Book of Constitutions*, a copy of which we were all given on the night of our Initiation, we find the following:

"The Charges of a Free-Mason.
Extracted from the antient records of lodges beyond the sea,
and of those in England, Ireland and Scotland.
To be read at the making of new brethren.
Published by order of the Grand Lodge."

First section entitled: Concerning God and Religion,

"A Mason is obliged, by his tenure, to obey the moral law; and if he rightly understands the art will never be a stupid atheist nor an irreligious libertine...A Mason is, therefore, particularly bound never to act against the dictates of his conscience...Masons unite with the virtuous of every persuasion in the firm and pleasing bond of fraternal love;...Masons strive, by the purity of their own conduct, to demonstrate the superior excellence of the faith they may profess."[19]

Having given us this great guidance for our relationship with our God, the Charge now teaches us the other obligations we have;

> "...as a citizen of the world..."

an obligation towards our Country and our community. It implores us to be;

> "...exemplary in the discharge of our civil duties, by never countenancing any act that may have a tendency to subvert the peace and good order of society."

As the *Book of Constitutions* explains under section II of the Antient Charges:

> "Masonry has ever flourished in times of peace and been always injured by war, bloodshed, and confusion; so that kings and princes, in every age, have been much disposed to encourage the craftsmen on account of their peaceableness and loyalty..."[20]

It is not therefore surprising that during the last war, while Hitler prepared for the invasion and occupation of England, Nazi Intelligence prepared a document entitled, *Sonderfahndanglist GB* or rather "Special Search List Great Britain". *(See illustration on page 80.)*

This list contained some 3,000 entries including the names of some prominent Freemasons and addresses of Masonic buildings as well as companies that had dealings with Freemasons, all of whom I have no doubt would have been singled out and subject to the humiliations known to be practised by that fearsome regime.[21]

That this fraternity should show such allegiance to one's King and country is another example of our antiquity. The building programmes of those gothic architects of the 12th–14th centuries depended much upon monies raised by great religious foundations, much through sponsorship from monarchs. Loyalty to one's sponsor would have been demanded and one would have been reliant upon them for their livelihood as well as protection.

It may also be worth noting that all trade guilds accepted men not engaged in their particular craft as patrons or as a means of bestowing an honour or special privilege. Royal patronage was not uncommon as Edward

III, Henry IV, Henry VI and Henry VIII were all guild members.[22] In a world where many countries have dismantled their monarchy and turned republic, the United Grand Lodge of England stands immovable in its open and unashamed displays of loyalty to our Sovereign, and brethren both young and old stand perfectly upright and erect as we affirm that loyalty during each Lodge meeting by respectfully singing the national anthem.

With regard to our domestic duties, the Charge now shows us the characteristics needed to adequately discharge them. I will quote from those wonderful Craft lectures which these days remain an important point of reference, yet I am sorry to say are rarely referred to.

*"**Temperance** – Is that due restraint of our passions and affections which renders the body tame and governable, and relives the mind from the allurement of vice. This virtue ought to be the constant practice of every Freemason, as he is thereby taught to avoid excess, or the contracting of any vicious or licentious habits, whereby he might unwarily be led to betray his trust, and subject himself to the penalty contained in his Obligation."*

*"**Fortitude** – Is that noble and steady purport of the soul, which is equally distant from rashness or cowardice; it enables us to undergo any labour, pain, danger or difficulty, when thought necessary or deemed prudently expedient. This virtue, like the former, ought to be deeply impressed in the breast of every Freemason, as a fence and security against any attempt which might be made either by threats or violence, to extort from him any of those Masonic secrets he has so solemnly engaged to hele, conceal and never improperly reveal, the illegally revealing of which might prove a torture to his mind"*

*"**Prudence** – Teaches us to regulate our lives and actions according to the dictates of reason, and is that habit of mind by which wise men judge, and prudentially determine, all things relative to their temporal and eternal welfare. This virtue ought to be the distinguishing characteristic of every Free and Accepted Mason, not only for the better regulation of his own life and actions, but as a pious example to the popular world who are not Freemasons, and should be nicely attended to in all strange or mixed company, never to let drop of slip the least sign, token, or word, by which any of our masonic secrets might be illegally obtained."*

*"**Justice** – Is that station or boundary of right which teaches us to render every man his due, and without distinction. This virtue is not only consistent with Divine and humans laws, but is the standard and cement of civil society; without the exercise of this virtue, universal confusion would ensue, lawless force overcome the true principles of equity, and social intercourse no longer exist; and as justice, in a great measure, constitutes the really good man, so it ought to be the invariable practice of every Freemason never to deviate from the minutest principles thereof..."*

And so on to those two truly Masonic ornaments which we are counselled, should be maintained in their fullest splendour, and are second only to Brotherly Love, in the three Grand Principles that the Order was founded upon namely, Benevolence and Charity.

William Preston had the following to say upon this subject:[23]

"The most inveterate enemies of Masonry must acknowledge, that no society is more remarkable for the practice of charity, or any association of men more famed for disinterested liberality. It cannot be said, that Masons indulge in convivial mirth, while the poor and needy pine for relief. Our charitable establishments and quarterly contributions, exclusive of private subscriptions, to relieve distress, prove that we are ready, with cheerfulness, in proportion to our circumstances, to alleviate the misfortunes of our fellow-creatures..."

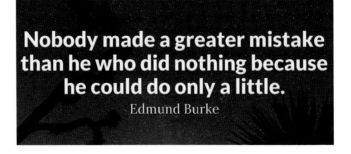

Nobody made a greater mistake than he who did nothing because he could do only a little.

Edmund Burke

> *"Possessed of this amiable, this godlike disposition, Masons are shocked at misery under every form and appearance. When they behold an object pining under the miseries of a distressed body or mind, the healing accents which flow from the tongue mitigate the pain of the unhappy sufferer, and make even adversity, in its dismal state, look gay. When pity is excited, they assuage grief, and cheerfully relieve distress. If a brother be in want, every heart is moved; when he is hungry, we feed him; when he is naked, we clothe him; when he is in trouble, we fly to his relief. Thus we confirm the propriety of the title we bear; and convince the world at large, that BROTHER, among Masons, is more than the name."*

And in another brother's view:

> *"Charity means shortly – and particularly in Freemasonry – all round good-will, beneficence, kindness and service for and to others, to bear the cross, if needs be, for others wrong doing, to do unto others, etc, knowing that these form the only* [characteristic] *which will procure admission into the Grade Lodge above."*[24]

I need not here dilate any further upon this subject only to say that charity is the most godly of all attributes we can obtain and practice. There is scarcely a Masonic publication, book, magazine or lecture that does not touch upon it, and in biblical terms it is second only to that first and great commandment: Love the Lord thy God.

Moving on, our attention is peculiarly and forcibly directed towards three other great excellences, Secrecy, Fidelity and Obedience.

Secrecy. The secrecy that we practice is simply no longer secret. Wilfully perjured individuals have chosen to reveal so much of our ceremonies to the world that we scarcely have any secrets left. However, passing from what secrets we have, and on to why we have secrets, we find that the skill of the medieval Operative Mason and any trade for that matter, are his secrets. The word mystery is derived from the Latin word "*ministerium*" meaning professional skill, therefore this ancient usage of the term mystery and secrets were actually of trade origin. Today, it is the modes of recognition that become our secrets, not the terms or handshakes for which we are renown, but the manner in which they are ritually taught and applied within the context of our ceremony. The demand for secrecy also forms part of the Obligations we take, and therefore we are obliged to maintain that characteristic in all our undertakings.

Fidelity. Fidelity is faithfulness, constancy and allegiance. It is one of those terms that encompasses all of the major tenets of the Craft in one word. It implies devotion and piety and, in the Masonic sense, to move forward slowly and steadily, learning, while affording appropriate respect to each degree and examining the true motives of those that wish us to sponsor their membership in the Craft.

Obedience. If love is the first commandment of heaven, and faith the first principle, then obedience is the first Law, such is the importance of this characteristic. It pervades our entire Craft journey, it illustrates our submission to the Master and his Wardens and it shows our willingness at all times to undergo examination. Obedience creates order, and a harmonious Lodge is built upon order. Therefore, in showing obedience we demonstrate that respect due to the Officers of the Craft, its principles and landmarks as well as its laws and bye-laws. In essence obedience brings a peacefulness to all of our proceedings.

In its closing comments, the Charge exhorts us to follow such pursuits that will at once make us recognisable as a Freemason and a useful ornament to mankind and to this society, this needs no further illumination on my part.

We are also encouraged to make a daily advancement in Masonic knowledge and I would suggest there has never been a better time to do so. We not only have access to knowledge through our masonic museums and libraries, but through Lodges of Research, magazines, Internet web-sites and regularly published books. Study is an important part of Masonry. Through study we learn, absorb and apply. Through study we not only become better masons, but better husbands, fathers and citizens of the world that we may ever have imprinted upon our hearts the sacred dictates of Truth, of Honour, and of Virtue.

Note A)

Mencius is the Latinised form of Meng-tzu, the man whom the Chinese call the "The Second Sage" who lived 372-289 BC. He based his entire system of thought on the concept of *jen*; humaneness and benevolence to which he also added the concept of *i*, righteousness and duty.

<h2 style="text-align:center">Note B)</h2>

Taken from the Prestonian Lecture for 1986, entitled *The Old Charges*, by Wallace McLeod as a tentative reconstruction of the standard original version of the *Old Charges* in modern spelling.

<h3 style="text-align:center">The Admonition before the Charge</h3>

Every man that is a Mason take right good heed to these charges, if that you find yourselves guilty in any of these, that you may amend you against God. And especially ye that are to be charged, take good heed that ye may keep these charges, For it is a great peril for a man to foreswear himself upon a book.

<h3 style="text-align:center">The Charges General</h3>

1) The first charge is that ye shall be true to God and the holy Church; and that ye use no error nor heresy, by your understanding or by discreet or wise men's teaching.

2) And also that ye shall be true liege men to the king without treason or falsehood; and that ye know no treason or treachery, but that ye amend it if ye may, or else warn the King or his council thereof.

3) And also ye shall be true each one to another; that is to say, to every Master and Fellow of the Craft of Masonry that be Masons allowed, ye shall do to them as ye would they should do to you.

4) And also that every Mason keep true counsel of Lodge and of chamber, and all other counsel that ought to be kept by the way of Masonry.

5) And also that no Mason shall be a thief or thief's fere, as far forth as he may know.

6) And also that ye shall be true to the lord and master that ye serve, and truly to see to his profit and advantage.

7) And also you shall call Masons your Fellows or Brethren, and no other foul name; nor you shall not take your Fellow's wife in villainy, not desire ungodly his daughter nor his servant.

8) And also that ye pay truly for your meat and drink where you go to board.

9) And also ye shall do no villainy in that house whereby the Craft may be slandered.

The Collected Prestonian Lectures 1975–1987, p283-284.

<h2 style="text-align:center">Note C)</h2>

Earliest known Speculative Charge, found in W. Smith's *Pocket Companion*, dated 1735.

A SHORT
CHARGE
To be given to new admitted
BRETHREN

You are now admitted by the unanimous Consent of our Lodge, a fellow of our most Antient and Honourable Society; *Antient*, as having subsisted from times immemorial, and *Honourable*, as tending in every Particular to render a Man so that will be but comfortable to its glorious precepts. The greatest Monarchs in all ages, as well of *Asia* and *Africa* as of *Europe*, have been Encouragers of the *Royal Art*; and many of them have presided as *Grand Masters* over the *Masons* in their respective Territories, not thinking it any lessening to their Imperial Dignities to Level themselves with their Brethren in Masonry, and to act as they did.

The World's great *Architect* is our *Supreme Master*, and the unerring Rule he has given us, is that by which we Work.

Religious Disputes are never suffered in the Lodge; for as Masons, we only pursue the universal Religion or the Religion of Nature. This is the Cement which unites Men of the most different Principles in one sacred Band, and brings together those who were the most distant from one another.

There are three general Heads of Duty which Masons ought always to inculcate, *viz.*, to *God*, our *neighbours* and *ourselves*.

To God, in never mentioning his Name but with that Reverential Awe which becomes a Creature to bare to his Creator, and to look upon him as the *Sumum Bonum* which we came into the World to enjoy; and according to that View to regulate all our Pursuits.

To our Neighbours, in acting upon the Square, or doing as we would be done by.

To ourselves, in avoiding all Intemperences and Excesses, whereby we may be rendered incapable of following our Work, or led into Behaviour unbecoming our laudable Profession, and in always keeping within due Bounds, and free from all Pollution.

In the State, a Mason is to behave as a peaceable and dutiful Subject, conforming chearfully to the Government under which he lives.

He is to pay due Deference to his Superiors, and from his Inferiors he is rather to receive Honour with some Reluctance, than to extort it.

He is to be a Man of Benevolence and Charity, not sitting down contented while his Fellow Creatures, but much more his *Brethren*, are in want, when it is in his Power (without prejudicing himself of Family) to relieve them.

In the Lodge, he is to behave with all due Decorum, lest the Beauty and Harmony there of should be disturbed or broke.

He is to be Obedient to the Master and presiding Officers, and to apply himself closely to the Business of Masonry, that he may sooner become a Proficient therein, both for his own Credit and for that of the Lodge.

He is not to neglect his own necessary Avocations for the sake of Masonry, nor to involve himself in quarrels with those who through Ignorance may speak evil of, or ridicule it.

He is to be a Lover of the Arts and Sciences, and to take all Opportunities of improving himself therein.

If he recommends a Friend to be made a MASON, he must vouch him to be such as he really believes will conform to the aforesaid Duties, lest by his Misconduct at any time the Lodge should pass under some evil Imputations. Nothing can prove more shocking to all faithful MASONS, than to see any of their *Brethren* profane or break through the sacred Rules of their Order, and such as can do it they wish had never been admitted.

Note D)
William Preston's Charge at Initiation into the First Degree, *Illustrations of Masonry*, 1812 Edition.
The paragraphs enclosed in brackets [ ] may be occasionally omitted, if time will not admit of delivering the whole Charge

BROTHER [As you are now introduced into the first principles of our Order, it is my duty to congratulate you, on being accepted a Member of an ancient and honourable Society; ancient, as having subsisted from time immemorial; and honourable, as tending, in every particular, so to render all men who will be conformable to its precepts. No institution was ever raised on a better principle, or more solid foundation; nor were ever more excellent rules and useful maxims laid down, than are inculcated on every person when he is initiated into our mysteries. Monarchs in all ages have been encouragers and promoters of the Art, and have never deemed it derogatory from their dignities, to level themselves with the brethren, to extend their privileges, and to patronise their assemblies.]

As a Mason, you are to study the moral law, as it is contained in the sacred code; (In England, the Bible; but in countries where that book is unknown, whatever is understood to contain the will or law of God.) to consider it as the unerring standard of truth and justice, and to regulate your life and actions by its divine precepts.

The three great moral duties, to God, your neighbour, and yourself, you are strictly to observe:– To God, by holding his name in awe and veneration; viewing him as the chief good, imploring his aid in laudable pursuits, and supplicating his protection on well-meant endeavours: – To your neighbour, by acting upon the Square, and, considering him equally entitled with yourself to share the blessings of Providence, rendering unto him those favours, which in a similar situation you would expect to receive from him:– And to yourself, by not abusing the bounties of Providence, impairing the faculties by irregularity, or debasing the profession by intemperance.

In the state, you are to be a quiet and peaceable subject, true to your sovereign, and just to your country; you are not to countenance disloyalty or rebellion, but patiently submit to legal authority, and conform with cheerfulness to the government under which you live; yielding obedience to the laws which afford you protection, and never forgetting the attachment you owe to the place of your nativity, or the allegiance due to the sovereign or protectors of that spot.

[In your outward demeanour you are to avoid censure or reproach; and beware of all who may artfully endeavour to insinuate themselves into your esteem with a view to betray your virtuous resolutions, or make you swerve from the principles of the institution. Let not interest, favour, or prejudice, bias your integrity, or influence you to be guilty of a dishonourable action; but let your conduct be uniform, and your deportment suitable to the dignity of the profession.]

Above all, practice benevolence and charity; for these virtues have distinguished Masons in every age and country. [The inconceivable pleasure of contributing toward the relief of our fellow-creatures, is truly experienced by persons of a humane disposition; who are naturally excited, by sympathy, to extend their aid in alleviation of the miseries of others. This encourages the generous Mason to distribute his bounty with cheerfulness; by supposing himself in the situation of an unhappy sufferer, he listens to the tale of woe with attention, bewails misfortune, and speedily relieves distress.]

The Constitutions of the Order are next to engage your attention. [These consist of two points, oral and written communication. The former comprehends the mysteries of the Art, and are only to be acquired by practice and experience in the Lodge; the latter includes the history of genuine Masonry, the lives and characters of its patrons, and the ancient charges and general regulations of the Craft.]

A punctual attendance on the duties of the Order we earnestly enjoin, more especially in that assembly where your name is enrolled as a member. [There, and in all regular meetings of the fraternity, you are to behave with order and decorum, that harmony may be preserved, and the business of Masonry properly conducted. The rules of good-breeding you are never to violate, by using unbecoming language, in derogation of the name of God, or toward the corruption of good manners: neither are you to enter into any dispute about religion or politics; or behave irreverently, while the Lodge is engaged in what is serious and important.] On every occasion you are to pay a proper deference and respect to the Master and presiding officers, and diligently apply to the work of Masonry, that you may sooner become a proficient therein, as well for your own credit, as the honour of the company with whom you associate.

Although your frequent appearance at our regular meetings be earnestly solicited, your necessary employments are not to be neglected on that account: neither are you to suffer your zeal for Masonry to exceed the bounds of discretion, or lead you into argument with persons who may ridicule our system; but extend your pity toward those who may be apt through ignorance to contemn, what they never had an opportunity to comprehend. All that is required for your general observance is, that you study the liberal arts at leisure, trace science in the works of eminent masters, and improve in the disquisitions of the system, by the conversation of well-informed brethren, who will be equally ready to give, as you can be to receive, instruction.

Finally; Adhere to the constitutions, and support the privileges which are to distinguish you as a Mason above the rest of the community, and mark your consequence among the Fraternity. If, in the circle of your acquaintance, you find a person desirous of being initiated into the Order, be particularly attentive not to recommend him, unless you are convinced he will conform to our rules; that the value of Masonry may be enhanced by the difficulty of the purchase; the honour and reputation of the institution established on the firmest basis; and the world at large convinced of its benign influence.

[From the attention you have paid to the recital of the duties of the Order, we are led to hope that you will form a proper estimate of the value of Freemasonry, and imprint on your mind the dictates of truth, honour, and justice.]

References / sources

1) From a statement adopted by Grand Lodge on 12th September 1962 and re-issued in the Extracts from the proceedings of the Quarterly Communications of Grand Lodge of 9 December 1981.

2) *Emulation Ritual*, 1991 edition, p67.

3) *Ibid*, p71-72.

4) *Ibid*, p73-74.

5) John T. Thorp, *The Origin and Antiquity of Masonry, British Masonic Miscellany*, compiled by George M. Martin, vol 1, p57.

6) *British Masonic Miscellany*, compiled by George M. Martin, vol 8, p133.

7) Wallace McLeod, *The Old Charges, The Collected Prestonian Lectures 1975–1987*, p261.

8) Harry Carr, *The Charge To The Initiate, The Freemason At Work*, p232.

9) *Emulation Ritual*, 1991 edition, p98.

10) *Ibid*.

11) *Ibid*, p98-99.

12) *Ibid*, p99

13) *Ibid*.

14) Frederick Smyth, *A Reference Book For Freemasons*, p293-4.

15) H. F. Inman, *Masonic Problems and Queries*, p228.

16) *Ibid*, p90.

17) *Emulation Ritual*, 1991 edition, p99.

18) *Aldersgate Ritual*, 1969 edition, p68.

19) *Book of Constitutions*. 1965 edition, p3.

20) Ibid, p4.

21) Mike Martin, *Why is Freemasonry so Secret in Britain*, p4.

22) M. Lawrence, *Stealing History*, p4.

23) M. M.Taylor, *Lectures on Freemasonry*, First lecture, Section Six

24) William Preston, *Illustrations of Masonry*, 1812 edition, p17-19.

25) A. Holmes-Dallimore, *Freemason's All in All* – p249

The story of the apron from its instigation in the Garden of Eden to its association with the Craft

"...more ancient...more honourable..."

(Written in 2004)

Throughout the world today, the apron has become one of the universal symbols of the Freemason, probably only second by association to that of the square and compasses, but this humble working man's garment has a unique place in the heart of every Freemason, but despite this association with Freemasonry, the Entered Apprentices' plain white apron has been worn by many early cultures and civilisations.

For example, initiates of the Mithras and Essenes cultures wore white leather aprons, as did the ancient initiates of the early Chinese societies. Both Jewish and Druidical High Priests were adorned by the white apron as were the early Anglican clergy and early Christians at their baptism. Mayans, Incas, Aztecs, Hopi, Vikings, and Zulu's wore white aprons as emblems of high office, while white aprons decorated statues of Greek and Egyptian Gods. The Persians also used the apron as a national emblem.

In fact, its origins can be traced back to the days of Father Adam and Mother Eve, for when their eyes were opened and they realised their own nakedness they sewed together fig leaves and made themselves aprons and as a result of his fall, Adam's penalty, so Genesis, Chapter 3 tells us, was expulsion from the garden and to till the ground. Of course, had he not ate the fruit, then in the garden he would have remained forever, never to learn about, or to receive the rewards bought by hard work. Therefore, the principle of work is associated with the apron and this concept is as old as time itself.

The apron, like our gloves and gauntlets, are a further link in the evolutionary chain, demonstrating our intimate association with the ancient operatives of the Craft. The aprons of the operatives consisted of skins of considerable size, tied around the waist by a leather strip or thong from each side which were split into strips and when tied and reached down to the ankles. All had a turn over, flap or bib at the top, the position of which

disclosed the status of the worker. For example, the Apprentice wore his flap turned up, possibly tied around his neck, the Fellow of the Craft wore his turned down inside, while the Master wore his turned down outside.

The earliest representation of a Masonic apron we can definitely claim as in the speculative sense occurs, I am advised, on a portrait of Anthony Sayer, the first Grand Master, 1717.

With regard to the white leather used, a very practical point soon made itself felt, which led to the refinement and adornment of the simple leather apron. Undyed white leather was very apt to leave white marks on the clothing of the brethren and this led to the provision of a lining.

In the Minutes of 17 March 1731, Grand Lodge we read the following:

"...that all those who have served in the Grand Offices shall wear their white leather aprons lined with blue silk. That those brethren who have served as Stewards shall wear their aprons lined with red silk, and the Master and Wardens of Lodges shall wear their aprons lined with white silk."

This is the earliest mention of the colour blue in connection with Masonic clothing, but we do not get any indication of the shade of blue until 1734, when on the authority of the Deputy Grand Master an order was given for Masonic clothing. This was described as:

"Two Grand Master's aprons lined with Garter blue silk and turned over two inches, with white strings; two deputy Grand Master aprons turned over one inch and a half, ditto." Here we arrive at a definite shade of blue, the Garter blue, and there is no possibility of doubt about the appearance on the fronts of the aprons, which from the modest turnover binding of the edges, has developed into the borders on the aprons which we now have.

It must be noted that the Garter blue used was not the colour which we recognise by that name today. In Stuart times, the Garter ribbons were light sky-blue, similar to that on Craft aprons today. This was the original Grand Officers colour. It was not until about 1745 that George II altered the shade of Garter blue to the darker colour we are now accustomed. This was in order to distinguish his Garter Knights from those supporters of James II and his heirs who had been created Knights of the Garter by the exiled family, and were not recognised by the Hanoverians.

When this alteration to the darker shade of blue of the Garter took place, the aprons of the Grand Officers followed suit and so still remain today as Garter blue. The light blue was left available for the Craft in general and in time was adopted at the Union in 1813.

Why was blue chosen? Possible because of three verses in Numbers 15:

38 *"Speak unto the children of Israel, and bid them that they make them fringes in the borders of their garments throughout their generations, and that they put upon the fringe of the borders a ribband of blue:"*

39 *"And it shall be unto you for a fringe, that ye may look upon it, and remember all the commandments of the Lord, and do them; and that ye seek not after your own heart and your own eyes..."*

40 *"That ye may remember, and do all my commandments, and be holy unto your God."*

The first mention of gold fringes was in 1787, and is found on the bill received for the apron of the Prince of Wales and the Duke of York. Both aprons cost £1-1s-0d, £1.05p in today's money.

Prior to any kind of uniformity, aprons came to be of all sorts of sizes, colours and materials. Those of the *'Antients'* were larger and longer than those of the *'Moderns'* and Brethren began to adorn them with beautiful Masonic designs, either embroidered, embossed or painted, the more elaborate the better. This practice finally reached a situation where aprons became too costly for ordinary men in ordinary Lodges.

*c.*1752   1791

The strings of the aprons which had received the embellishment of decorated ends, were passed around the waist and tied under the fall of the flap so the tasselled ends would hang down on the front of the apron.

The seven metal tassels on our Craft aprons today were adopted as a permanent decoration in 1813 and we are told remind us that no Lodge is perfect unless seven Brethren are present: The Master, his two Wardens, two Fellowcrafts and two Entered apprentices. We also learn that in older times, the seven ages of man were thought to be influenced by the seven then known planets and no Master Mason was considered efficient unless he had some knowledge of the seven liberal arts and sciences. These tassels ultimately became attached to two vertical ribbons representing the two pillars at the porch way or entrance to King Solomon's Temple.

In addition to this, rosettes and levels or taus, which indicate the rank of the wearer, were added as a regulation pattern again in 1813, along with the size which is generally 14-16in wide and 12-14in deep. The Rosettes and the levels or taus are set in the form of a triangle with the apex upwards, symbolical of the Divine Life attainable by complete knowledge after the resurrection. The levels have also been said to represent the first, second and third step in regular Freemasonry.

In older times, the apron was made from lamb skin and before it can be made, the life of an animal must be taken. That animal, the lamb, has ever been regarded as the symbol of innocence and therefore the apron is regarded as symbolic of peace and innocence.

To close this first section, I will just clear up the issue of the aprons "snake" clasp.

The snake or serpent has no association with Freemasonry or our symbolism. Opponents of Freemasonry have made every effort to use this as evidence that Freemasons worship the snake/serpent, representative of Satan.

Navel Brigade 1871

It was in use long before it the regalia makers adopted this simple pattern or belt fastening that had previously been used for military and police uniforms.

By far the most amusing reference to aprons can be found in Laurence Dermott's *Ahiman Rezon* where he says of the "Moderns":

> *"There was another old custom that gave umbrage to the young architects, i.e., the wearing of aprons, which made the gentleman look like mechanics, therefore it was proposed that no brother should wear an apron. This proposal was rejected by the oldest Members, who declared that the aprons were all the signs of Masonry then remaining amongst them, and for that reason they would keep and wear them. It was then proposed, that as they were resolved to wear aprons they should be turned upside down, in order to avoid appearing mechanical. This proposal took place, and answered the design, for that which was formerly the lower part, was now fastened round the abdomen, and the bib and strings hung downwards, dangling in such manner as might convince spectators that there was not a working mason amongst them.*
>
> *Agreeable as this alteration might seem to the gentlemen, nevertheless it was attended with an ugly circumstance: for, in traversing the lodge, the brethren were subject to tread upon the strings, which often caused them to fall with great violence, so it was thought necessary to invent several methods of walking, in order to avoid treading upon the strings.*
>
> *After many years' observation on these ingenious methods*

of walking, I conceive that the first was invented by a man grievously afflicted with the sciatica. The second by a sailor, much accustomed to the rolling of a ship. And the third by a man who, for recreation or through excess of strong liquor, was wont to dance the drunken peasant."

In bringing this short paper to a close, every Freemason will recall those words spoken to him by the Senior Warden on the night of his initiation, *"...more ancient than the Golden Fleece or the Roman Eagle and more honourable than the Garter..."* Actually, these names were highly respected contemporary civil Orders.

Philip, Duke of Normandy founded the Order of the Golden Fleece in 1429. As wool was the predominate product of the lower European countries the fleece was chosen as the emblem. It is considered as the highest of all civil Orders in Europe

In 1701, Frederick I of Prussia founded the Order of the Black Eagle. The number of knights was limited to 30, exclusive of the Princes of royal blood. The revisers of our rituals probably selected the reference to the Roman Eagle as it was the highest emblem of dignity, honour and power that famous empire could bestow.

According to tradition in 1343, Edward III was dancing with the Countess of Salisbury when he picked up a garter that had slipped from her leg and placed it about his own. At this time the King had been successful in his campaigns and he therefore instituted an Order for rewarding his army favourites. After a series of changes by ensuing monarchs the Order became known as The Most Noble Order of the Garter.

Now, as you cast your mind back to the night of you own initiation, remember you apron is:

- The badge of innocence, because it is the skin of the lamb, the age old symbol of innocence.
- The bond of friendship, referring the fraternal bond of Freemasonry and the first of the three grand principles on which the Order was founded – Brotherly Love.
- More ancient than the Order of the Golden Fleece, founded in 1429, and the Roman Eagle, referring to the Order of the Black Eagle, founded in 1701, because that device can be traced back to time immemorial.
- More honourable than the Most Noble Order of the Garter, because it has been earned by your own industry.

Therefore, always remember that old adage, "Wear your apron with pride".

References / sources
A. Holmes-Dallimore, *The Freemasons all in all*
H. F. Inman, *Masonic Problems and Queries*
M. Hoath, *The Apron! A Distinguishing Badge of a Mason*
R. F. Gould, *The History of Freemasonry*

What Every Entered Apprentice Should Know At His Passing

(Written in 2005)

On the night of our initiation and within about 15 minutes of being instructed that we should "endeavour to make a daily advancement in Masonic knowledge" we send our Initiate on his merry way with nothing but a *Book of Constitutions*, a copy of the Lodge Bye-Laws, and a set of test questions to learn, in preparation for his next step, and what's more, the poor chap is seldom given any guidance on where to find that Masonic knowledge to make his daily advancement. In fact, it was only when I spoke to a young Entered Apprentice who explained to me how difficult it was to read the *Book of Constitutions* that I realised how we had let him down.

Thus, came the inspiration for this piece of work.

You see, if we are asking a person to answer a series of questions as proof of his proficiency and giving him the answers in such a simplified form, then he has done no more than learn the answers rather than understand the questions, and as today's Lodges of Instructions are more likely to be Lodges of Rehearsal, where else can an Entered Apprentice really learn the answers to the questions?

Some might suggest that his Proposer or Seconder may assist, but I am sad to say in my experience many are not always able themselves to offer an adequate response and in some cases, pass on incorrect information, albeit unintentionally. I therefore felt some urgency in my desire to help the many Entered Apprentices that I meet to gain a greater understanding of their first steps in Masonry.

With this objective in mind, I have used the 11 questions put by the Master, to the Candidate, on the night of his being passed to the degree of a Fellow Craft. It is the answers to these questions that determine one's competency in that previous degree and all I have done is to illuminate those answers as the starting point for the beginning of one's daily advancement.

My explanation in thus:

1) Q. Where were you first prepared to be made a Mason?
A. In my heart.

This is a perfectly reasonably response, for as we labour to meet the needs and desires of our heart, this is where each Mason should first feel the desire to join our fellowship. In a similar manner, as the heart is that life giving organ which we singularly pledge so carefully to our loved ones, so this pledge to Masonry is both sincere and true. Therefore, it is our heart that we should open to prepare to receive the wonderful gift of brotherhood.

2) Q. Where next?
A. In a convenient room adjoining the Lodge.

The convenient room adjoining the Lodge is of course the Tyler's room, that small anti-chamber generally situated in the North-West corner. This is where each Candidate undergoes the preparation for his entry into masonry. In not so well-appointed buildings any room situated near the Lodge room can be used. It is also here we find the Tyler or Outer Guard, generally in the form of an experienced, mature brother who cheerfully puts us at ease as he helps us prepare. Armed with a drawn sword, his role is symbolically to keep off all intruders and Cowan's to masonry.

3) Q. Describe the mode of your preparation?
A. I was divested of metal and hoodwinked. My right arm, left breast and knee were made bare, my right heel slipshod and a cabletow placed about my neck.

We are **divested of metal** for three especial reasons which we learn later in the ceremony. These reasons are:

Firstly – *to put our principles to the test.* We are taught that charity is the distinguishing characteristic of a Freemasons heart; therefore, the universal principles of beneficence are awakened in us immediately when the Master offers us the opportunity to exercise that ideology. Unfortunately, our situation at that point precludes us from gratifying our desires, but our willingness to do so, if circumstances permitted, is acknowledged.

Secondly – *to evince to the brethren that we have neither money nor metallic substance about us.* Traditionally this is an illusion to the building of King Solomon's Temple where we read in: **1 Kings 6:7** "And the house, when it was in building, was built of stone made ready before it was brought thither: so that there was neither hammer nor axe nor any tool of iron heard in the house, while it was in building."

King Solomon's Quarry

The Lodge room here where we meet, as we know, is representative of King Solomon's Temple.

Thirdly – *as a warning to our heart of that peculiar moment we were received into masonry, poor and penniless.* This stands as a reminder that should we by chance, at a future time, meet a friend or brother in a distressed situation who might solicit our assistance, then we will recall ourselves when we were received into Freemasonry both poor and penniless and we cheerfully embraced that opportunity of practising that virtue we professed to admire.

The **hoodwink** placed upon us represents the darkness of ignorance and has its place in many age-old rituals. It enables us to reflect more upon the new life we are about to enter, i.e. from darkness to light. It also ensures that our heart may conceive before our eyes shall discover. We may also consider that if we have had a change of mind, it serves as a shield and prevents us seeing the formation of the Lodge room before having taken the Obligation, whereupon we can be led out of the room. It should also remind us to keep the entire world from our mysteries.

Lastly, it acts as a test of the faith we had previously acknowledged at our interview, in the Great Architect, ever knowing that where His name is invoked no harm will befall us.

Our **right arm** was made bare to show we are ready for labour. Likewise, our **left breast** is made bare to show that we carry no concealed weapon. Of course, it is of paramount importance that nothing offensive or defensive is brought into the Lodge to disturb its harmony and here is an opportunity for the Tyler to ensure that the candidate is not an intruder or Cowan. Many also consider it confirms the gender of the candidate, although I do not necessarily subscribe to that theory. Finally, it shows that we are prepared to discover the secrets and mysteries with an open heart.

We have our **left knee** made bare, for it is upon that knee we kneel to take the Great and Solemn Obligation. The left was once considered the sacred side of the body, which coincides with the teaching of the Matriarchal Age, for the left is supposed to be feminine and the right masculine. Jason, the leader of the Argonauts, in the quest for the Golden Fleece, came before Pelias without a shoe on his left foot. Vervain, used by the Druids in casting lots, was dug up with the left hand. The Caduceus, the magical wand, was carried by Hermes in his left hand.

We are **slipshod** because among the ancient traditions of the east there were two Jewish practices. Firstly, it was custom to slip off a shoe as a pledge of fidelity. We can find reference to this in the book of **Ruth 4:7-8,**

7: *"Now this was the manner in former time in Israel concerning redeeming and changing, for to confirm all things; a man plucked off his shoe, and gave it to his neighbour: and this was a testimony in Israel."* 8: *"Therefore the kinsman said unto Boaz, buy it for thee. So he drew off his shoe."* This was a gesture of honesty, sincere intention and an affirmation of an agreement made between two parties. Many also consider it confirms the Initiate is a free man and not wearing manacles. Again, I do not necessarily subscribe to that theory.

A **cabletow** is placed about our neck. This small length of cable is used for towing, hauling or safeguarding against too much speed on a strong current. It was customary among the ancient Semitic races for captives, bondmen and other menials to wear a halter as a token of submission. The Candidate can therefore demonstrate the act of perfect acquiescence. It was also used by the Druids, Brahmins, and Greeks in their religious ceremonies and in our setting, it acts as a restraint, rendering any attempt by the candidate to rush forward, fatal.

4) Q. *Where were you made a Mason?*
A. *In the body of a Lodge, just, perfect and regular.*
Here is our first introduction to three most important Landmarks of the Order. A Lodge is considered **"Just"**, when the Volume of Sacred Law lies open on the Masters pedestal. **"Perfect"**, when seven or more regularly made Freemasons are present. **"Regular"**, when the Warrant or Charter of the Lodge, issued by the United Grand Lodge of England, is on display.

In March 1877, the Grand Orient of France made alterations to its Constitutions which excluded amongst other things, the Volume of Sacred Law from its ceremonies, this meant that their Lodges could no longer be considered **"Just"** and this action transgressed one of the most important Landmarks of the Order.

In December 1877, a special committee of the Grand Lodge of England was appointed to consider the matter and submitted their report to Grand Lodge on 6 March 1878. Subsequently, the Grand Lodge of England withdrew all recognition from the Grand Orient of France.

Thus, Freemasons who are members of Lodges constituted under the Grand Lodge of England are not at liberty to attend any such Lodge constituted under the Grand Lodge of the Orient, known as an irregular Grand Lodge.

The seven that make a Lodge **"Perfect"** are "…the Master and his two wardens…two fellow crafts…two Entered Apprentices…" Seven or more make a perfect Lodge, because King Solomon was seven years and upwards in building, completing, and dedicating the Temple at Jerusalem. They have likewise a further allusion to the seven liberal Arts and Sciences. Seven appears repeatedly throughout the Bible and is considered to be a powerful and mystical number.

- God rested on the seventh day after completing the work of the creation.
- Jacob bowed seven times before his brother Esau to show perfect submission.
- God ordered the lamp stand or (Menorah) should have seven branches.
- The feasts of the Lord lasted seven Sabbaths.
- The land was divided into seven lots.
- There were seven loaves that filled seven baskets.

These are just a few of the numerous references to the number seven found in the Bible.

In the medieval period, a Cathedral was deemed **"Regular,"** if it was part of a monastery. The clergy were monks who lived and conducted their lives by the strict monastic rule of whichever the Order they were part of. They took little notice of what was happening in the outside world and kept themselves entirely to themselves. History shows us that in many cases when Masons arrived ready for work, houses were sometimes built for them and they tended to keep themselves in tight little communities and were  probably looked upon by the locals as suspicious strangers.

In today's Craft, our work and business is kept strictly within the realms of our "Regular" Lodges which are deemed so by the Warrant that each

Lodge carries. The warrant is representative of the Monarchs authority issued in this form to working Lodges or companies of masons who were actively plying their trade and proof that they were bona fide tradesmen.

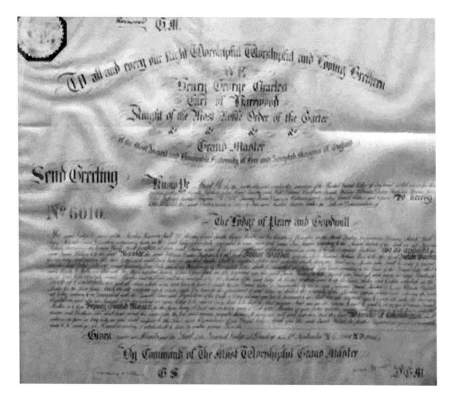

5) Q. And when?
A. When the sun was at it meridian.
The Sun being that great luminary which guides man's path by day and reaches its meridian at high noon, at this time during the day, the activities of the Operative Lodge would have been in full swing, thus indicating by this answer that the Lodge was open and at labour.

6) Q. In this country Freemasons' Lodges are usually held in the evening; how do you account for that which at first view appears a paradox?
A. The earth constantly revolving on its axis in its orbit round the sun and Freemasonry being universally spread over its surface, it necessarily

follows that the sun must always be at its meridian with respect to Freemasonry.

In reality, this question purely goes to point out that masonry is universal and technically speaking, at any given time around the world, there would be at least one speculative Lodge at labour.

7) Q. What is Freemasonry?
A. A peculiar system of morality, veiled in allegory and illustrated by symbols.
- A peculiar system of morality – A distinctive practice of decency
- Veiled in allegory – Disguised in parables
- And illustrated by symbols – And demonstrated by images.

Any good dictionary or thesaurus will give you an explanation of this sentence in a slightly different wording but meaning the same and Freemasonry is no less than this.

Morality or decency, I really do not need to dilate here other than to say we all know the levels of behaviour and conduct that makes man unique. That is to say in all the animal kingdom, man alone can knowingly raise his standards to those expected by that Great Architect of the Universe to whom we acknowledge as our Creator and Overseer.

> THE MOST IMPORTANT ENDEAVOR IS THE
> STRIVING FOR MORALITY IN OUR ACTIONS. OUR
> INNER BALANCE AND EVEN OUR VERY EXISTENCE
> DEPEND ON IT. ONLY MORALITY IN OUR ACTIONS
> CAN GIVE BEAUTY AND DIGNITY FOR LIFE.
>
> ALBERT EINSTEIN

Since the dawn of time **allegory or allegorical** story-telling by way of parables, analogies or tales have been employed to teach, train and help man to understand an important or salient point. Man could communicate by mouth, long before he could read and many of the world's most ancient histories were related in this form before any other means.

The power of **symbols or images** teach man in an even-handed manner, for each sees the same. I believe it was Thomas Aquinas, that Dominican Friar, of the 13th century who said "…man cannot understand without images…" In a similar fashion, Richard Taylor, author of *"How to read a Church"* believes that there are three characteristics of an image or symbol:

i) They can express concepts that language cannot.

ii) They can bridge gaps where language can be too difficult.

iii) They can touch us at a depth that wordy exposition does not.

Thus, like allegory, symbols have been employed since the dawn of time to educate man.

8) Q. Name the grand principles on which the Order is founded?
A. Brotherly Love, relief and truth.

The term "**brotherly love**" extends to the manner in which we treat each other which should be in a most respected manner. By this means, we should support a brother in all of his laudable undertakings, keep his lawful secrets when entrusted to us and support his character in his absence as well as his presence. The term **relief** encompasses our attitudes towards the whole of mankind, for no Freemason should ever turn his back on any poor soul in need of assistance where it was in his capacity to help. **Truth** stands for honesty, integrity, loyalty and fidelity, those attributes that should be about us in all of our daily undertakings. These should be the characteristics that set us apart from the world, that when people judge Freemasonry, and they will, they will look upon it favourably.

9) Q. Who are fit and proper persons to be made Masons?
A. Just, upright and free man, of mature age, sound judgement, and strict morals.
The terms, "**just and upright**" needs no further amplification; however I am drawn to our old lectures to explain the term "**free**": *"It alludes to that grand festival given by Abraham at the weaning of his son Isaac, when Sarah, Abraham's wife, observing Ishmael, the son of Hagar, the Egyptian bond-woman, teasing and perplexing her child, remonstrated with her husband saying, "Put away that bond-woman and her son, for such as they shall not inherit with my son, even with Isaac." She spake as if endued with a prophetic spirit, well knowing that from the loins of Isaac would spring a great and mighty people, such as would serve the Lord with freedom, fervency, and zeal; and fearing that if the two youths were brought up together that Isaac might imbibe some of the slavish principles of Ishmael, it being a general remark in those days, as in the present, that the minds of slaves were less enlightened, and more contaminated than those of the Free. This is the reason that Freemasons give why all men should be free-born; but, in the present day, slavery being generally abolished, it is considered that if a man be free, although he may not be free-born, he is still eligible to become a Freemason"*

In the Constitutions of 1723 it was stated that no man should be made a Mason under the age of 25 years unless by dispensation from the Grand Master. In the Constitutions of 1784 it was changed to 21 years. However, it was the practice of Lodges constituted under the Grand Lodge of the "Antients" to reserve the mature age as being that of 25 years. This however was finally resolved at the Union in 1813 when the minimum age became

21. Again, I consider that the terms **"sound judgement"** and **"strict morals"** need no further illumination as they are both self-explanatory.

10) Q. How do you know yourself to be a Mason?
A. By the regularity of my initiation, repeated trials and approbations. And a willingness at all times to undergo an examination when properly called on.

You will recall from an earlier question that the term **"regular"**, when applied to Freemasonry, refers to the manner in which the Lodge has been constituted. All Lodges issued with warrants under the United Grand Lodge of England are therefore **"regular"**. Members of **"regular"** lodges are not permitted to attend any Lodge that has not been duly constituted in this manner or those considered by definition to be irregular. Advice should be sought from you own Lodge secretary before visits to Lodges in other parts of the world.

At our **initiation**, and after having taken the great and solemn obligation of a Mason, we were given three especial things; a sign, a token and a word.

A **sign**, which was an allusion to a penalty which a Mason would rather suffer than improperly disclose the secrets entrusted to him.

A **grip or token**, which when regularly given or received goes to distinguish a brother by night as well as by day.

A **word**, which is so highly prized amongst Masons that too much caution cannot therefore be observed in its communication, it should never be given at length but always by letters of syllables.

It was immediately after receiving these that we underwent our first trial and approbation, firstly, in the South of the Lodge, when the Junior Deacon presented us to the Junior Warden and then secondly, to the West of the Lodge when the Junior Deacon presented us to the Senior Warden. On both these occasions we underwent a trial or test while receiving the approbation or approval of those two Principal Officers of the Lodge, when we answered their respective question correctly.

Being prepared to **"undergo an examination when properly called upon"** is required particularly when visiting other Lodges where we are not known. The Junior Warden of that Lodge, as the ostensible Steward, may ask us to prove ourselves a mason, at which point he will ask us for that sign, token and word.

After this trial or strict examination, he will grant his approbation thereby allowing us to enter a Lodge of Entered Apprentices. It is not required or expected for an Entered Apprentice to visit any other Lodge unless specifically invited to do so by a well-known brother of that Lodge who can personally vouch for you.

Invitations such as this are only generally made on the night of another initiation ceremony that we are at liberty to attend by virtue of the Degree that we hold, that we can more fully observe the ceremony. The modes of recognition are reserved exclusively for use in the context of Lodge room only and we will never be expected or never should we demonstrate them, outside of that situation.

11) Q. How do you demonstrate the proof or you being a Mason?
A. By signs, tokens, and the perfect points of my entrance.
A chance discovery of a scrap of paper known as the Harliean fragment and dated by the British Museum at about 1650 is the first known allusion to English Masonic words and signs and says the following: *"There is several words and signs of a free mason to be revealed to you which as you will answer before God at the great and terrible day of judgement...you keep secret and not to reveal the same to any in the ears of any person but to the masters and fellows of the said Society of Free Masons so help me God."*

We have already learnt the importance of these modes of recognition, what they are and when they will be expected to be used. Let me confirm that they will never be expected of us outside of that Masonic setting. There are three distinct possibilities that one could consider that the phrase **"perfect points of my entrance"** refers to when demonstrating he is a Mason:

    i) his Entrance as a Candidate
    ii) his Entrance into Freemasonry
    iii) his Entrance into a Lodge at work

The First Lecture, First Section, seems to point to all three for we have this exchange:
    W.M. Will you give me the points of entrance?
    CAN. If you give me the first I will give you the second.
    W.M. I hele.
    CAN. I Conceal.
    W.M.. What is it that you wish to conceal?
    CAN. All secrets and mysteries of or belonging to, Free and accepted Masons in Masonry.

W.M. This being open Lodge, what at other times you wish to conceal may now safely reveal?
CAN. Of, at, and on.
W.M. Of, at, and on what?
CAN. **Of** my own free will and accord. **At** the door of the Lodge. **On** the point of a sharp implement presented to my naked left breast.

Of my own free will and accord, indicating his entrance into Masonry. **At** the door of the Lodge, indicating his entrance into a Lodge at work. **On** the point of a sharp implement presented to my naked left breast, indicating his willingness to undergo such trials and approbations to prove his membership or entrance into Freemasonry. The perfect points of one's entrance then being – **Of, At and On.**

On a closing note, I cannot reiterate the point or speak to strongly about the education of our people; neither can I impress upon each of us the importance of making a daily advancement in Masonic knowledge. Maintaining the lifelong interest in our noble science does not happen automatically, we must teach, train and encourage our candidates to understand the true principles of Masonry and the joy found in the fellowship of our fraternity. Therefore, the use of the following mediums is positively encouraged:

The Internet – This has become the most popular method of bringing Masonic information into our homes. There are literally thousands of web sites throughout the English-speaking world, all freely available at the touch of a button and what's more, if you do not have a computer at home, try your local library. One word of caution however, there are official and unofficial Masonic websites, but almost all Grand Lodges throughout the world have their own and I suggest these are the first sites you review.

Magazines – The beauty of magazines, like the web sites, is that you can read the views and articles of several different people and these articles are often followed up by letters shedding more light or a different view point on the subject. They are inexpensive and often run series of articles on one subject. You also have news, reviews and topical features.

Books – The biggest drawback of books is the cost, which in some cases are prohibitive. They also only present one person's view point and if you do not enjoy the book, you have wasted your money. A quick check in the review columns of Masonic magazines will help you in that department.

Lodges of Research – There are not many subjects in Freemasonry that have not been exhaustively covered by these associations, and their research is first class. If you are the type of person who enjoys anything with a Masonic flavour, particularly deep intellectual articles, then the Lodge of Research is for you.

Finally, not everything you read or find that is labelled "Masonic" is in truth, actually Masonic, and we live it a society which tolerates the views of all people. Therefore, you will find much false information about Freemasonry as you carry out your studies. My only advice to you is to ensure you encompass your studies with *bona fide* material from good reliable sources, and whether you decide to log on to those web sites, subscribe to a magazine, build your own library or join a Lodge of Research, the only true way to make that daily advancement in Masonic knowledge is a conscious commitment to regular study.

A look at the similarities that existed within the ritual practices of early 19th century American Freemasonry and the pre-1940 ceremonies of The Church of Jesus Christ of Latter-day Saints

Did Freemasonry Influence Mormonism?

(Written in 2006)

"The secret of Masonry is to keep a secret"
Joseph Smith Jr, History of the Church, Vol 6 p59

In the annals of anti-Masonic history, one group of people stand alone in their claim that the practices carried out in Masonic Temples, though apostate, are close enough to be directly descended from the ritual and ceremony practised in King Solomon's Temple. These people, the Church of Jesus Christ of Latter-day Saints, often referred to as Mormons, claim to have received ceremonies by revelation which bare close resemblance to that of the three degrees of Craft Freemasonry and the Holy Royal Arch. Since the introduction of their ceremonies and rituals, many critics of the church have argued that no such revelation was received and their practices are based entirely upon the ceremonies and rituals previously established by Freemasonry.

The scope of this paper is to explore the suggestion that Joseph Smith, founded of the Church, and other early Mormon Church leaders, modified and used Masonic ritual for their own purpose. I intend to compare these parallels by examining the following:

- The origins of the Masonic ritual.
- The revelations revealing these ceremonies to Joseph Smith.
- The Masonic membership of early church leaders.
- The similarity in signs and grips.
- The Five Points of Fellowship.
- The ceremony of Passing the Veils.

This paper therefore is not intended to be a general exposé of either Mormon or Masonic practices, but rather an examination of printed material which has all been found within the public domain. Having explained my intention, I firmly, yet fairly believe that a stance of sanctity or secrecy, coupled with associated penalties, should not deter people from the facts or hide the truth by keeping people in darkness. Therefore, by necessity, I have found it impossible to proceed with this paper without making reference to certain ceremonial and ritualistic practices, but by using previously published material, I have endeavoured to respect the sanctity of the Mormon faith, the covenants I once made in the Mormon Temple at Lingfield, Surrey, and the Obligation of fidelity I have taken as a Freemason.

This paper also carries a warning that it contains explicit material showing the Signs, Tokens and Words used in the pre-1940 Temple ceremonies of The Church of Jesus Christ of Latter Day Saints and the 1830 Lodge Rooms of America.

The Church Stands Accused

There is no lack of writings which accuse the Mormon church of blatant theft or imitating the Masonic ritual as the following quotes will show. For example, Past Grand Master S. H. Goodwin wrote the following:

> *"The observant Craftsman cannot be long among the Mormon people without noting the not infrequent use made of certain emblems and symbols which have come to be associated in the public mind with the Masonic fraternity. And now and again he will catch expressions and phrases in conversation, and meet with terms in literature, which are suggestive, to say the least. If he should continue his residence in Utah, he will sometimes be made aware of the fact, when shaking hands with a Mormon neighbour or friend, that there is a pressure on the hand as though some sort of "grip" is being given."[1]*

Other writers like Charles Kelly and Hoffman Birney, have been much more scathing in their remarks:

> *"The Prophet's (Joseph Smith) attitude upon being expelled from Masonry was apparently that he had been kicked out of better places and he promptly transferred the ceremonies of his clandestine lodge to Mormonism, adding all the new frills and furloughs he had received from Yahweh. He converted the Masonic apron to a union suit, and from Masonry appropriated its grips, five points of fellowship,*

> *much of its symbolism and almost the exact phraseology of certain masonic Passages."[2]*

Further observations regarding the temple ritual of the Mormons were made by J. H. Beadle:

> *"The general outline is evidently modelled upon the Mysteries or Holy Dramas of the Middle Ages. Much of it will be recognised as extracts from Morgan's Freemasonry Exposed, by those familiar with that work; and the origin of this is quite curious...Smith's New Translation of the Old Testament is full of anti-Masonry; the fifth chapter of Genesis as he has it, which is added entire to our version, is devoted entirely to the condemnation of secret societies, and sets forth particularly how they were the invention of Cain after "he fled the presence of Lord..."*
>
> *Some years after, however, the Mormons all became Masons and so continued until they reached Nauvoo; there Joseph Smith[3] out-Masoned Solomon himself and declared that God had revealed to him a great key-word, which had been lost, and that he would lead Masonry to far higher degrees, and not long after their charter was revoked by Grand Lodge. How much of Masonry proper has survived in the Endowment, [4] the writer will not pretend to say; but the Mormons are pleased to have the outside world connect the two and convey the impression that this is celestial masonry."[5]*

Another writer Stuart Martin expresses his opinion in a similar manner:

> *"Even the endowment scene in the Temple ceremonies is not original, as some readers may have noticed. Over and over again one is confronted with situations and incidents in the ceremony which bear a strong resemblance to those used in Masonry; and it has been stated that when Joseph Smith and Sidney Rigdon were beginning their crusade they were not sure what to preach, but were influenced not a little by an anti-masonry campaign which was then very popular in America. The general outline of the endowment ceremony, and the signs*

> *used therein are closely connected with Masonry; and, in spite of Mormon denials, it is easily established that a certain amount of the early Masonry was used freely in the Temple ceremony still survives."[6]*

In a letter to E. Cecil McGavin,[7] Mr S. A. Burgess, Historian of the Reorganised Church Of Jesus Christ of Latter-Day Saints[8] wrote the following:

> *"The Utah Church, on one hand, denies the connection between their Temple ceremonies and Free Masonry, yet several who were Masons before entering the Temple have noted a marked similarity. Also, some at least, tell that Joseph Smith perceived that the purity of the ritual had been restored, and that is what is used in the Temples in Utah."*

In a further publication from the Reorganised Church we read the following:

> *"It is evident to any reader, from a description of the ceremonies used in the Mormon temples (and so many have told of them they are no longer secret), that they are adopted largely, if not altogether, from the Masonic Lodge. The Masonic Lodge of Utah has issued pamphlets denouncing the Utah temple ceremonies as clandestine Masonry, and giving that as a principal reason for denying the right of any Mormon to join the Masonic Lodge in Utah.*
>
> *Brigham Young was a mason in Nauvoo, and it appears that he introduced the Masonic ritual into his temple ceremonies.*
>
> *It is a well-known fact that he made the Bee Hive a prominent emblem in his work, even making it the State emblem. The Bee Hive, the garments[9], the apron, the All-Seeing eye, the constellation, and the square and compass on the garments and in the temples were all taken bodily from the Masonic Lodge. The grips, signs, and penalties are similar."[10]*

C. A. La Rue states that after Grand Lodge revoked the Nauvoo Lodge Charter:

> *"Smith then denounced Masonry as an unholy institution of the Priesthood and proceeded to invent his endowment rite which he called the true Masonry known to Seth and Solomon.*

He began to administer these rites over his brick store in a room he had prepared at Nauvoo."[11]

From another source, we read yet more of the same testimony:

"On March 15, 1842, the Mormon leaders joined the Masonic lodge, in spite of Masonry being bitterly condemned in their scriptures. That event changed the essential nature of Mormonism by converting it into a mystery cult. The Masonic emblem and ritual were converted into what the Mormon historian frankly calls the "Masonic sacred drama of the fall of man." A Mormon temple is not a church but a "grand Masonic fabric," in which religious truth is presented in symbolism. Furthermore the principles of Masonic hierarchy were adopted. Joseph preached: "The keys are certain signs and words by which the false spirits and personages may be detected from the true, which cannot be revealed to the Elders till the Temple is completed....There are signs in heaven, earth and hell; the Elders must know them all, to be endowed with power, to finish their work and prevent imposition. The devil knows many signs but does not know the sign of the Son of Man, or Jesus." On 9 February 1843, Joseph revealed "three grand keys," for detecting the nature of a heavenly being, but left some "keys" unrevealed, since he died before the temple was completed. About seven weeks after joining the lodge Joseph began to give instructions on the ancient order of the keys, washings and anointing's, and endowments, and it appears that twelve thousand Mormons went through those rites in Nauvoo. This Masonic ritual, it was explained, was revealed by an angel, and the Prophet only joined the lodge to see what extent it had degenerated from its Solomonic purity. Furthermore there is best evidence for believing that Joseph taught that Masonic principles and practices operated among the gods as well as on earth. His followers in Utah were taught, that there is a sort of divine masonry among the angels who hold the priesthood, by which they can detect those who do not belong to their order. Those who cannot give the signs correctly are supposed to be impostors...

Smith's love of parade was not unrelated to his membership

in the Masonic lodge, and if he went a little farther than the
small-town lodge man it must be remembered that he was less
hampered by criticism..."[12]

As a final quote to this section I use the words of Edward Tullidge in his
book *The Life of Joseph the Prophet*:

"He understood that the chain of Masonry is the endless chain
of brotherhood and priesthood, linking all the worlds – the
heavens and the earths – but he believed that this earth had
lost much of its purpose, its light, its keys, and its spirit, – its
chief loss being the key of revelation. For instance, his
conception might be expressed in the statement that the
Masonic church on earth ought to be in constant
communication with the Masonic church in the heavens,
notwithstanding its many nations, races, religions,
civilisations, and law-givers."[13]

From these quotes, it is more than evident that Mormon ceremonies, carried
out in their Temples, were and are similar to the Masonic ritual performed
in their Temples, now more regularly called Lodge rooms.

Chronologically, Freemasonry is 113 years older that the Mormon
Church and although both often claim greater antiquity in their origins, the
fact remains that from official records we know that Grand Lodge of
England was formed in 1717,[14] whereas the Church of Jesus Christ of
Latter-Day Saints was established in 1830.[15]

Joseph Smith the Mason

Records show us that Joseph Smith, Snr, was initiated into Masonry in the
Ontario Lodge No 23, Canandaigua, New York, on 26 December 1817,
being passed on 2 March 1818 and raised on 7 May 1818. His son Hyrum,
Joseph's older brother, was a youth member of Mount Moriah Lodge No
112, Palmyra, New York, although his personal records appear to be
missing.[16]

Of course, there is some debate as to the first given name of Hyrum and
critics have sported the idea that Smith Snr was influenced by the Hiramic
legends of Freemasonry. However, I must dispute the idea as Hyrum was
born on 9 February 1800, some 17 years before Smith Snr was initiated in
to Masonry.[17]

Other eminent Mormons who were Freemasons prior to joining the church were Newel K. Whitney, Heber C. Kimball, John C. Bennett, George Miller, Lucius N. Scovil, Elijah Fordham, John Smith, Austin Cowles, Noah Rogers and James Adams.[18] It was in fact these brethren that openly encouraged Joseph to seek membership in Freemasonry. Having said that, Joseph Smith Jnr. may well have also been influenced at the time by the Masonic works of people like the Rev George Oliver (1782–1867) who described the order with such sagacity that it would appeal to most men:

> *"Masonry works daily without noise, regarding all Brethren with love and honour; not asking one which system he follows, nor another the colour of his decoration, or how many degrees he has, but judging only from his works; not minding what his business may be, or what sect he belongs to, but if he be a faithful workman whose example may be followed. Thus will Freemasonry increase, the different systems and forms will vanish, and the true fraternity form a chain of Truth and Light."[19]*

Who could not fail to be drawn towards such an organisation which boasted such bonds of love and fraternity? And in a similar vein:

> *"By the exercise of brotherly love we are taught to regard the whole human species as one family, the high and the low, the rich and the poor, who, as created by one Almighty parent, and inhabitants of the same planet, are to aid, support and protect each other. On this principle, Masonry unites men of every country, sect and opinion and causes true friendship to exist among those who might otherwise have remained at a perpetual distance."[20]*

Looking at the backdrop of Joseph Smith's life since forming the new church in 1830, both he and its members had undergone great persecution from mobs. They were quite literally chased out of Fayette, New York,[21] Kirtland, Ohio,[22] Jackson County, Missouri,[23] and eventually Nauvoo, Illinois.[24] However, it was in Nauvoo that he became a Mason.[25]

> *"When Installing Nauvoo Lodge, Grand Master Abraham Jonas made Joseph Smith, Jr and his immediate administrative associate, Sidney Rigdon, each a Mason at sight, March 15-16, 1842."*

The general consensus of opinion among writers is that Joseph and his associates sought such membership in an effort to gain some form of protection for the church members.

> *"Who are the friends of Masonry?" inquires one who knew the answer. "Generals and Presidents, Magistrates and Clergy, Lawyers, Doctors and Statesmen, good men and true. Number the stars if you can, or the sands upon the sea shore, then count the friends of Masonry."*[26]

Their city at Nauvoo was growing both in size and influence and they were a power to be reckoned with. It was felt that the brethren in the Lodges of Illinois would have found this allegiance as mutually beneficial. Besides these reasons, I spoke to a High Priest of 30 years standing in the Church who explained that according to the official church history, Joseph himself was commanded by the Lord to join Freemasonry. Although at this time I do not have a reference to substantiate this fact. Smith himself would have been no stranger to Freemasonry at that time. His father, brother, and many friends were members of the Craft. In fact, since the *Morgan affair*[27] of 1826, there had been a wave of anti-Masonic feeling throughout the land which lasted till 1845.[28] This appeared to have had no effect on Smith or his associates, and the Nauvoo Lodge can lay claim to having initiated into Masonry the first five presidents of the Mormon church, namely:[29] Joseph Smith 1830–1844, Brigham Young 1847–1877, John Taylor 1880–1887, Wilford Woodruff 1887–1898, and Lorenzo Snow 1898–1901.

It was not long after the formation of the Nauvoo Lodge that Grand Master Abraham Jonas started to receive complaints. For example, in five months the Lodge had initiated 256 candidates and raised 243.[30] In fact, Mervin Hogan claims that the Lodge had as many as 1,529 members.[31] Needless to say its charter was rescinded, yet despite this the Lodge continued to work.[32]

The Antiquity of Masonic Ritual

Before we examine the all-important question of ritual similarity and to what extent Joseph Smith and the church was influenced (if in fact it was) by Masonry, we must explore the antiquity of both sets of ritual.

Ritual, by our own general understanding, is an established form of ceremony or observance carried out in a solemn or respectful manner. We generally associate it with religious liturgy or those other formal occasions.

The Collins dictionary presents us with four good definitions of the word:
1) The prescribed or established form of a religious or other ceremony
2) Such prescribed forms in general or collectively
3) Stereotyped activity or behaviour
4) Any formal act, institution, or procedure that is followed consistently.

I think it fair to say Freemasonry consistently practices an established form of ceremony; therefore we can actually call it ritual as opposed to a rite which, according to the same source, refers purely to religious liturgy. Some theorists believe that the ritual was not composed or invented, but was the perpetuation of the activities, practices and usages of the daily work and customs of operative stonemasons or Cathedral builders. It was not known as ritual, but was called work. Others argue that it came about through people such as Dr James Anderson, John Desaguliers, Laurence Dermott and later William Preston who modernised some of the old practices and introduced innovations or new workings.

What we do know is that the current tri-gradal or three-degree Craft system, with its allegorical associations with Solomon's Temple and the death of its Chief Architect, Hiram Abiff, was introduced into the ceremony between 1724–1730, and were designed specifically to illustrate the salient points of our discipline, being fidelity, obedience and secrecy, and is no more than a fictional or romantic story, grammatically incorrect and historical inaccurate.

The general consensus of opinion being the degrees, a term not used until about 1730, of Entered Apprentice and Fellowcraft were formulated prior to the Master's degree which was believed to have been introduced between 1711 to 1725 (*The Freemason At Work*, Harry Carr, p357). The degrees were performed speculatively, in the back rooms of ale houses prior to the dedicated Lodge rooms being established. They were continually modified until the early 19th century when they were formalised by the Lodges of Promulgation and Reconciliation, before and after the Act of Union of 1813.

Operative Masons had grades rather than degrees:
• Masters: Men who made contracts and undertook the work of building for employers.

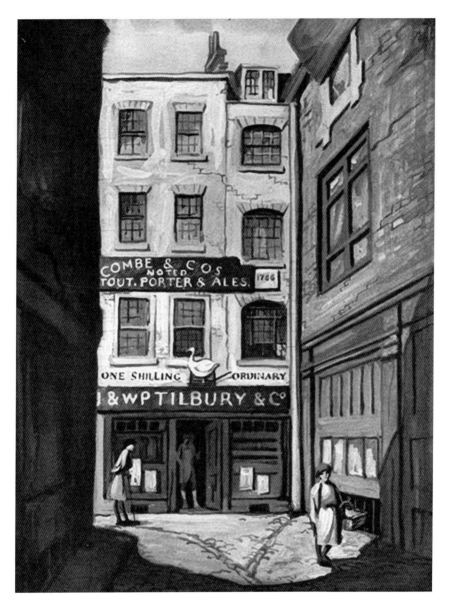

The Goose and Gridiron Ale house, St Paul's Church Yard, London,
where the first Assembly and Feast of the Free and Accepted Masons
was held on St John the Baptist's day in 1717.

- Fellow Crafts or Journeymen: Employed by the Masters to carry out the work.
- Entered Apprentices: Who were received that they might be taught the art of building.

Again, referring to that publication by Harry Carr, *The Freemason At Work*, p357, we read that evidence points to a two grade/degree system, i.e. that of Entered Apprentice and Fellow Craft (or Master), as early as 1598/99, but these were in fact Scottish trade related grades. The first record of the conferment of the third degree on a non- operative, speculative or Free and Accepted Mason was not until 1725. Bro Carr takes pains to point out that these dates indicate ceremonies that were practiced and not dates of introduction.

Much of the ritual and lectures were based on the early catechetical style of the old *MS Constitutions* which were trade based documents dating from the 14th century. We must also bear in mind that the early 16th century grades were operative in application moving to a speculative or non-operative nature by the 17th century.

Unfortunately, Freemasonry has always been fair game for writers and historians to introduce fabulous theories to connect Freemasonry with groups like the Italian *Roman Colligia*, the *Commacine Masters*, the German *Steinmetzens*, the French *Compagnonnage*, the English *Druids*, the *Ancient Greek Mysteries*, the *English Trade Guilds*, the *Knight Templars*, the *Monks of dissolved English Monasteries*, and other well-known esoteric and theosophical groups. All these at varying times may have had some influence on the early beliefs concerning the origin or development of Freemasonry, but these are all fictional and fanciful theories for which there is no formal evidence to prove any connection.

Therefore, the so-called mysteries of Freemasonry do not and never have existed in the form that many have imagined. For example, in England during the middle-ages it became the practice to call the trade skill of any artisan, 'a mystery'. This being taken from the Latin word "ministerium" meaning professional skill, thus it is unrealistic to believe this is reference to the ancient mysteries of past civilisations. This phrase purely relates to the secrets of the working man's art or skill.

It was particularly unfortunate that Joseph Smith and his many contemporaries would have considered Masonic ritual to be descended from Solomon's Temple itself, like a kind of ancient priesthood that had degenerated. This, of course, was nothing new as the general consensus of opinion at the time, judging by the many books written on the subject, was that Freemasonry was hundreds, if not thousands, of years old, not helped by Andersons 1734 Constitutions which gave a history of the Craft right back to Adam.

Smith felt that God had revealed to him a great key-word and he felt he could lead Masonry to far higher degrees; such was his misunderstanding of Freemasonry. This would explain why the Nauvoo Lodge proved so popular in its short time of existence and why it had so many Mormon initiates. It may have been considered, at that time, essential for their salvation.

Masonic ritual itself, with its lectures and practices was not formally established until as late 1813. I choose the date 1813 carefully as this was the date of the Act of Union, when the first Grand Lodge, founded in 1717, and its rival Grand Lodge, founded in 1751, joined together and formalised its rituals and practises.

The main foundation for the study of early ritual in England is based on a group of four documents, three complete texts and a fragment:

- *The Edinburgh Register House* MS, 1696
- *The Chetwode Crawley* MS, *c.*1700
- *The Kevan* MS, *c.*1714
- *The Haughfoot fragment*, 1702

These documents, which because of their provenance have been deemed indisputable evidence, formed the basis for all Masonic ritual. Similarly, the legendary history of Freemasonry was taken from a tranche of what appear to be earlier Trade documents, in particular two specific documents dating from 1390 (*the Regius Poem*) and 1410 (*the Cooke* MS,) respectively.

Despite what may be read, discussed, believed or presumed, these are the definitive documents recognised by Masonic historians from a total of 113 manuscripts which collectively are known as the "Old Charges", the remaining documents not mentioned, are accepted to be hand written copies of those already mentioned.

Therefore, there are no other set of writings, undisclosed documents or mysterious artefact's or discoveries that can take the organisation of speculative Freemasonry further back than about 1620 were we read in the *Encyclopaedia of Freemasonry and Kindred Sciences* by Albert G. Mackey MD the following:

> *"The Account of James Gilder Mr William Warde & John Abraham wardens of the Company of Freemasons within the City of London beginning the first day of Julie 1619 And ending the day of Julie 1620 of all receipts & payments for & to the use the same company as followeth, viz".*

From the entries in this book it appears that besides the ordinary Freemen and Liverymen of this Company, there were other members who are termed in the books the Accepted Masons and that they belonged to a Body known as the Accepcon or Acception, which was an Inner Fraternity of Speculative or Non-Working Freemasons.

> *"They charge themselves also with Money Received of the Persons hereafter named for they're gratuities at they're acceptance into the Lyvery viz"* (here follow six names).

Among the accounts for the next year (1621) there is an entry showing sums received from several persons, of whom two are mentioned in the entry of 1620, "Att the making masons", and as all these mentioned were already members of the Company something further must be meant by this.

Any doubt about the practice of making non-working or speculative Masons was removed in 1646 when that great English antiquary Elias Ashmole (1617–1692) announced in his diary that:

> *"I was made a Free Mason at Warrington in Lancashire, with Coll: Henry Mainwaring of Karincham in Cheshire. The names of those that were then at the Lodge, Mr Rich Penket Warden, Mr James Collier, Mr Rich Sankey, Henry Littler, John Ellam, Rich Ellam & Hugh Brewer."*

Although not published until 23 years after his death, it contains this very interesting entry. The published version differs slightly from the original entry, which is now preserved in the Bodleian Library, however in an article by W. H. Rylands, printed in the *Masonic Magazine*, December 1881, Bro Rylands shows that that all seven brethren mentioned were non-operative or non-working Masons.

On a final point of this section, Freemasonry is not a religion, participation in its rituals and ceremonies have never been essential to one's salvation, although a belief in God still forms part of the entry criteria and is recognised as one of the *Antient Landmarks of the Order.*

The Antiquity of Mormon Ritual

On 19 January 1841, Joseph Smith received the following revelation which some claim was the first time the Temple ritual was made known:

"For there is not a place found on earth that he may come to and restore again that which was lost unto you, or which he hath taken away, even the fullness of the priesthood...Therefore, verily I say unto you, that your anointing, and your washings, and your baptisms for the dead, and your solemn assemblies, and your memorials for your sacrifices by the sons of Levi, and for your oracles in your most holy places wherein you receive conversations, and your statutes and judgements, for the beginning of the revelations and foundations of Zion, and for the glory, honour, and endowment of all her municipals, are ordained by the ordinance of my holy house, which my people are always commanded to build unto my holy name.

And verily I say unto you, let this house be built unto my name, that I may reveal mine ordinances therein unto my people;

For I deign to reveal unto my church things which have been kept hid from before the foundation of the world, things that pertain to the dispensation of the fullness of times.

And I will show unto my servant Joseph all things pertaining to this house, and the priesthood thereof...."[33]

Although the Nauvoo Temple had yet to be built, the Temple in Kirtland, Ohio, did not work any such ordinances and Joseph Smith continued to reveal certain aspects of ceremonies that would be carried out in the holy place. Some nine months later, 3 October 1841, at a general church conference the following words were recorded:

"President Joseph Smith, by request of the Twelve Apostles, gave instructions on the doctrine of Baptism for the dead, which were listened to with intense interest by the large assembly....

The principle subject brought before the people at this conference was the redemption of the dead, and building the Temple. This matter appeared to impress itself upon the mind of Joseph with great force, and nothing, apparently, gave him more delight than to explain its importance to the saints.....He presented baptism for the dead as the only way that men can appear as saviours on Mount Zion."[34]

Baptism for the dead appears to be a New Testament practice and although there is just one quote concerning this subject, it is quite specific:

1 Corinthians 15:29 *"Else what shall they do which are baptised for the dead, if the dead rise not at all? Why are they then baptised for the dead?"* c.55-56 AD

The whole subject of Salvation for the dead again rests on one other specific scripture:

1 Peter 4:6 *"For this cause was the gospel preached also to them that are dead, that they might be judged according to men in the flesh, but live according to God in the spirit."*

However, supporters of this doctrine do lend other scriptures to substantiate their theory:

1 Peter 3:18-19 *"For Christ also hath once suffered for sins, the just for the unjust, that he might bring us to God, being put to death in the flesh, but quicked by the spirit: By which also he went and preached unto the spirits in prison:"* both scriptures c.64 AD.

Compare:

Isaiah 24:22 *"And they shall be gathered together, as prisoners are gathered in the pit, and shall be shut up in the prison, and after many days they shall be visited."*

Isaiah 42:6-7 *"I the Lord have called thee in righteousness, and will hold thine hand, and will keep thee, and give thee for a covenant of the people, for a light of the Gentiles; .*

To open the blind eyes, to bring out the prisoners from the prison, and them that sit in darkness out of the prison house."

Isaiah 61:1 *"The spirit of the Lord God is upon me: because the Lord hath anointed me to preach good tidings unto the*

meek; he hath sent me to bind up the brokenhearted, to proclaim liberty to the captives, and the opening of the prison to them that are bound;" all Isaiah scriptures c.740-701 BC.

Job 33: 27-30 *"He looketh upon men, and if any say I have sinned, and perverted that which was right, and it profited me not;*

He will deliver his soul from going into the pit, and his life shall see the light.

Lo, all these things worketh God often times with man,

To bring back his soul from the pit, to be enlightened with the light of the living." date approximately 6th-4th BC.

Front and side elevations of the Kirkland Temple.

The Kirkland Temple, Ohio, dedicated on 27 April 1836. In his dedicatory prayer, the Prophet Joseph Smith said the Saints had built the Kirtland Temple so the Lord would have a place *"to manifest himself to his people"* *(*D&C 109:5*)*. Doctrine and Covenants, Section 110 records a fulfillment of that request; the Lord appeared and said that He accepted the temple as His. Three other heavenly messengers appeared shortly after the Savior. They restored important priesthood keys to the Prophet Joseph Smith and Oliver Cowdery.

One month after the general conference, an epistle from the Latter-Day Twelve Apostles went on to say:
> *"The Saints are growing in faith, and the intelligence of heaven is flowing into their understanding, for the spirit of the Lord is with them, and the Holy Ghost is instructing them in things to come...God requires of his saints to build Him a house wherein His servants may be instructed, and endowed with power from on high, to prepare them to go forth among the nations, and proclaim the fullness of the Gospel for the last time, and bind up the law, and seal up the testimony, leaving this generation without excuse, and the earth prepared for the judgements which will follow. In this house all the ordinances will be made manifest, and many things will be shown forth, which have been hid from generation to generation."*[35]

So, by the end of 1841, just a few short months before Smith became a Mason, full details of the Mormon temple ritual had still not been revealed by the Prophet, neither had the temple been completed. In fact, the first record there is of the endowment ceremony being revealed is 4 April 1842, less than one month after Joseph Smith's initiation into the Craft. Elder Orson Hyde wrote the following after receiving this ordinance.
> *"Before I went east on the 4th of April, last, we were in council with Brother Joseph almost every day for weeks. Says brother Joseph in one of those councils, "There is something going to happen; I don't know what it is, but the Lord bids me to hasten, and give you your endowment before the temple is finished." He conducted us through every ordinance of the holy priesthood, and when he had gone*

through with all the ordinances he rejoiced very much and says, "now if they kill me you have got all the keys, and all the ordinances, and you can confer them upon others, and the hosts of Satan will not be able to tear down the kingdom as fast as you will be able to build it up; and now," says he "on your shoulders will rest the responsibility of leading this people, for the Lord is going to let me rest a while."[36]

As one might imagine, there are no biblical evidence of any ritualistic practices as suggested by Joseph Smith's revelation being carried out in the Solomonic Temple and it is hard to see how ordinances like baptism for the dead could have been practiced in that Temple on Mount Moriah, as baptism became a requirement for one's entry into the Kingdom after the advent of Christ (John 3:5). Christ had yet to be born; Christianity had yet to be established. Likewise, the endowment ceremony or the like, is nowhere to be found, neither does there appear to be any modern day mention of the brazen laver, the Holy of Holies or the Ark of the Covenant with its attendant golden cherubs. These were also all part of the furnishings of the that wonderful building of old, which would no doubt have greatly impressed the Queen of Sheba on her visit and it is little wonder that one should read, "Its costliness and splendour became objects of admiration of the surrounding nations and its fame spread to the remotest parts of the then-known world."[37]

The origin of the Mormon Temple ritual does not therefore seem to have appeared before 1842.

Examining Those Similarities

Without a doubt, there are some striking resemblances in the pre-1940 Mormon Temple ritual when compared to the Masonic ritual of the 1830s. Many say they are too close to be a coincidence and the fact that Joseph Smith was a Mason would have given him an opportunity to access Masonic ritual. Additionally, Morgan's *Freemasonry Exposed* was available in New York, from about 1826 and contained explicit details of Masonic ritual.

The Mormon Endowment is presented in a large room representing earth, where both men and women are taken through a series of tableaux from the creation of man to his expulsion from the garden. They are then presented with the means by which they may gain re-entry to the presence of the Lord. These instructions are then repeated at the veil in question and answer or catechetical form and on completion they are welcomed into the Celestial room and the presence of God.

Masonic ritual is presented in a Lodge room representative of King Solomon's Temple, through a series of catechetical and allegorical exchanges culminating in an act of great fidelity, where ultimately the chief architect is slain, rather than reveal the true secrets of a Master Mason. That secret, which is the name of the true and Living God Most High, is subsequent recovered in the ceremony of the Holy Royal Arch.

In each, participants are given, under obligation or covenant, a series of grips, passwords and signs at each degree or level. It is within these tokens and signs that we find many similarities.

I will now present those likenesses using as a reference point the following,

1) *Freemasonry Exposed*, 1826.
2) *Temple Mormonism – Its Evolution, Ritual and Meaning*, New York, 1931,
3) *Mormon's, Masonry and the Morgan Affair* by K. H. Montgomery,
4) *Illustrations of Masonry*, Chicago, 1827,
5) *Ritual and Illustrations of Freemasonry*, Reeves & Turner, London *c*.1860

I am also indebted to Jerald and Sandra Tanner, authors of the "*Evolution of the Mormon Temple Ceremony: 1842–1990*", Salt Lake City, Utah, Lighthouse Ministry, 1990, and the following web-sites,

lds-mormon.com
christian-restoration.com
windysydney.blogspot.co.uk
brothomasblog.blogspot.com

all of which I accessed via the Internet.

The First Token of the Aaronic Priesthood and the Degree of an Entered Apprentice Freemason

The Oath or Obligation with its penalty

Mormonism: "*.....we will not reveal any of the secrets of this, the first token of the Aaronic priesthood; with its accompanying name, sign or penalty...Should we do so, we*

agree that our throats be cut from ear to ear and our tongues torn out by their roots..."
(*Temple Mormonism*, p18).

Freemasonry: *"...I will ... never reveal any part or parts, art or arts, point or points of the secret arts and mysteries of ancient Freemasonry ... binding myself under no less penalty than to have my throat cut across, my tongue torn out by the roots..."*
(*Freemasonry Exposed*, p21-22).

The Sign

Mormonism: The sign is made by bringing the right arm to the square, the palm of the hand to the front, the fingers close together, and the thumb extended. The Execution of the Penalty is represented by placing the thumb under the left ear, the palm of the hand down, and by drawing the thumb quickly across the throat to the right ear and dropping the hand to the side. (*lds-mormon.com*)

Freemasonry: The (*sign is made by*) by dropping the left hand carelessly; at the same time raise the right arm and draw the hand, still open, across the throat, thumb next the throat, and drop the hand perpendicularly by the side. These movements ought to be made in an offhand manner, without stiffness. (Italics added)
(Freemasonry Exposed, p104-105)

The Grip.

Mormonism: The Grip or First Token of the Aaronic Priesthood is made by clasping the right hands and placing the joint of the thumb directly over the first knuckle of the other person's hand.
(*lds-mormon.com*)

Freemasonry: The Grip of an Entered Apprentice Freemason is made by taking hold of each other's hands as in ordinary hand-shaking and press the top of your thumb hard against the first knuckle-joint of the first finger near the hand.

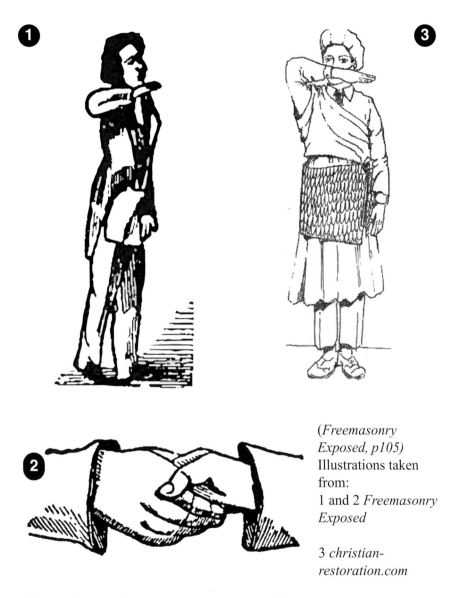

(*Freemasonry Exposed, p105*) Illustrations taken from:
1 and 2 *Freemasonry Exposed*

3 *christian-restoration.com*

The wording used during the presentation of the grip
　　Mormonism: A short discourse takes places, wherein the

participant takes the part of Adam. The guide or helper is Peter. Peter now takes Adam by the right hand and asks....
Peter. "What is that?"
Adam. "The first token of the Aaronic Priesthood."
Peter. "Has it a name?"
Adam. "It has."
Peter. "Will you give it to me?"
Adam. "I cannot, for it is connected with my new name, but this is the sign" (Temple Mormonism, p20).

Freemasonry: The Master and Candidate holding each other by the grip, as described, the Master asks...
Master. "What is this?"
Candidate. "A grip."
Master. "A grip of what?"
Candidate. "The grip of an Entered Apprentice Mason."
Master. "Has it a name?"
Candidate. "It has."
Master. "Will you give it to me?"
Candidate. "I did not so receive it, neither can I so impart it."
(*Freemasonry Exposed*, p23-24)

The Second Token of the Aaronic Priesthood and the Degree of a Fellowcraft Freemason

The Oath or Obligation with its penalty
Mormonism: *"...we and each of us do covenant and promise that we will not reveal the secrets of this, the Second Token of the Aaronic Priesthood, with its accompanying name, sign, grip or penalty. Should we do so, we agree to have our breasts cut open and our hearts and vitals torn from our bodies and given to the birds of the air and the beasts of the field....."*
(Temple Mormonism, p20).

Freemasonry: *"I.... most solemnly and sincerely promise and swear.... that I will not give the degree of a Fellow Craft*

Mason to anyone of an inferior degree, nor to any other being in the known world.... binding myself under no less penalty than to have my left breast torn open and my heart and vitals taken from thence ... to become a prey to the wild beasts of the field, and vulture of the air ..."
(*Freemasonry Exposed*, p52).

The Sign

Mormonism: The sign is made by placing the left arm on the square at the level of the shoulder, placing the right hand across the chest with the thumb extended and then drawing it rapidly from left to right and dropping it to the side.
(*Temple Mormonism*, p20)

Freemasonry: The sign is given by drawing your right hand flat, with the palm of it next to your breast, across your breast from the left to the right side with some quickness, and dropping it down by your side...
(*Freemasonry Exposed*, p53)

The Grip

Mormonism: The Grip is given by clasping the hand and pressing the thumb in the hollow between the first and second knuckles of the hand.
(*lds-mormon.com*)

Freemasonry: Take each other's hands as in ordinary hand-shaking and press the top of your thumb hard against the space between the first and second knuckles of the right hand.
(*Freemasonry Exposed*, p107)

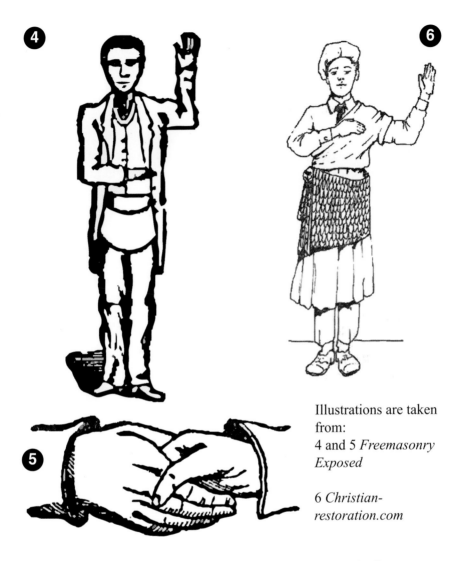

Illustrations are taken from:
4 and 5 *Freemasonry Exposed*

6 *Christian-restoration.com*

The First Token of the Melchizedek Priesthood and the Degree of a Master Mason.

The Oath or Obligation with its penalty

> **Mormonism:** "Should we (reveal these secrets), we agree that our bodies be cut asunder in the midst and all our bowels gush out."
> (*lds-mormon.com*)

Freemasonry: "...binding myself under no less penalty than to have my body severed in two in the midst, and divided to the north and south, my bowels burnt to ashes in the center, and the ashes scattered before the four winds of heaven..." (*lds-mormon.com*)

The Sign

Mormonism: "...The right hand is brought forward, the palm down, fingers close together, and the thumb extended. The thumb is placed over the left hip. The penalty is executed by drawing the thumb quickly across the body and dropping both *(hands)* to the side." *(Italics added)*
Mormon's, Masonry and the Morgan Affair by K. H. Montgomery, p5.

Freemasonry: The sign is made by dropping the left band carelessly and drawing the right across the body from left to right side on a line with the lower button of the vest, the hand being open as before, palm downward and the thumb towards the body. Then drop the hand perpendicularly to the side. (*Freemasonry Exposed,* p109)

Illustrations taken from:
7 *Freemasonry Exposed*

8 *Christian-restoration.com*

The sign of the Second Token of the Melchizedek Priesthood and the Grand Hailing Sign of Distress of Freemasonry

Mormonism: "...by raising both hands high above the head, palms forward, fingers closed together.."
Mormon's, Masonry and the Morgan Affair by K. H. Montgomery, p5

Freemasonry: "The sign is given by raising both hands and arms to the elbows, perpendicularly, one on each side of the head, the elbows forming a square.
Illustrations of Masonry, p76.

Illustrations taken from:
9 F*reemasonry Exposed.*

10 (overleaf) Photo taken from windysydney.blogspot.co.uk

In Masonry, we seldom see the ceremony of "passing the veils", however, in Mormonism, as in Solomon's Temple, the veil separates the Holy of Holies or the presence of the Lord. It is to the veil that the candidate for Endowment is brought to give proof of proficiency in what they have already learned. They are escorted to the veil where they are met by a sentinel, at which point of the ceremony and in order to exchange those grips and passwords, the candidate places his hands through cuts in the veil which are shaped like the square and compass. This culminates in the final answer which is exchanged in the following manner.

> **Mormonism:** "The five points of fellowship are given by putting the inside of the right foot to the inside of the Lord's, the inside of your knee to his, laying your breast close to his, your left hands on each other's backs, and each one putting his mouth to the other's ear, in which position the Lord whispers: "This is the sign of the token: "Health to the navel, marrow in the bones......." (*Temple Mormonism,* p22)

In Freemasonry, the same is conducted after the candidate, representing Hiram Abiff, is figuratively raised from the grave where he had been indecently interred after being slain by the three ruffians.

> **Freemasonry:** "He (the candidate) is raised on what is called the five points of fellowship ... This is done by putting the inside of your right foot to the inside of the right foot of the person to whom you are going to give the word, the inside of your knee to his, laying your right breast against his, your

left hands on the back of each other, and your mouths to each other's right ear (in which position alone you are permitted to give the word), and whisper the word Mahhah-bone ... He is also told that Mahhah-bone signifies marrow in the bone. (*Freemasonry Exposed*, pp84-85).

Illustrations taken from:
11 *Freemasonry Exposed*

12 (overleaf)
brothomasblog.blogspot.com

Other Similarities between pre-1940 Mormon practices and 1820's Freemasonry

Mormonism: The Patron removed all clothing and was clothed in a white undergarment.

Freemasonry: The Candidate was taken to a preparation or ante room, where all his clothes were removed and he was given a pyjama type set of clothes to wear.

Mormonism: The Patron was led to the veil of the temple, where the worker gave three distinct knocks with a mallet. Another worker asks from behind the veil, "What is wanted?"

Freemasonry: The Candidate was conducted to the door, where the conductor was caused to give, three distinct knocks, which were answered by three from within; the conductor gave one more, which was also answered by one from within. The door was then partly opened, and the Junior Deacon asked, "Who comes there? Who comes there? Who comes there?"

Mormonism: The Symbol of the compass was sown into the patron's garment over the left breast.
Freemasonry: The Senior Deacon pressed the point of a compass against the candidate's naked left breast.

Mormonism: The Patron put on a green apron "to cover their nakedness".
Freemasonry: The Entered Apprentice was given an apron of white lambskin as "an emblem of innocence".

Taken from *"Similarities between Freemasonry of the 1830s and the Mormon Endowment (pre-1940)"* By Richard Packham

The Mormon Response

It would be quite wrong of me to make any personal observations as to whether Freemasonry influenced Mormonism, as this is the prerogative of the reader. I must, however, in all fairness give the view of Mormon writers who have, over the years, defended the argument that there was any influence or connection between the two organisations.

> *"In the diary of Benjamin F. Johnson, an intimate friend and*
> *associate of Joseph Smith, it is recorded that 'Joseph told*
> *me that Freemasonry was the apostate endowment, as*

sectarian religion was the apostate religion.' Elder Heber C. Kimball, who had been a Mason for many years, related that after Joseph Smith became a Mason, he explained to his brethren that Masonry had been taken from the priesthood. "[39]

Apostle to the Church of Jesus Christ, Melvin J. Ballard has been quoted as saying the following:

"Modern Masonry is a fragmentary presentation of the ancient order established by King Solomon. From whom it is said to have been handed down through the centuries."

A quote from *The Salt Lake Herald* 29 December 1919:

"Masonry is an apostasy from the ancient early order, just as so-called Christianity is an apostasy from the true Church of Christ."

Again, from the pen of E, Cecil McGavin:

"Yes, there may be some similarities in the rituals ... In the light of the evidence supplied by Masonic historians, the conclusion is forced upon us that some of the features of the ritual once administered in Solomon's Temple have persisted in Masonry...Since some of the Masonic ritual has descended from Solomon's time, altered and corrupted by the passing centuries, should one be surprised to find a few similarities when the Temple ritual is again established. If the facts were available and the original sources extant, it would doubtless be apparent that everything in the ritual of the Mormons that the Masons say was taken from their ceremonies, dates back to Solomon's time." [40]

In sharp contrast to McGavins's statements we read the following:

"McGavin accepts the most fanciful claims to antiquity put forth by such discredited Masonic historians as Mackey, Anderson and Oliver. These early Masonic writers were wont to claim Solomon, Adam, and most of the upright men of the Old Testament as early lodge brothers. Modern Masonic historians date the origin of the lodge in the early eighteenth

> *century and recognize that these pioneer speculative Masons simply adopted the story of the building of Solomon's temple as a dramatic background for their initiations...A few elements in modern Masonry here and there can be traced to the medieval guilds of working masons, but no one with a scholarly reputation would try to maintain that the degree system as it is worked now – and as it was worked in Nauvoo in 1842 – could have possibly been derived from Solomonic rites."*[41]

As a close to this section I pose the following question. Why would Joseph Smith become a Mason? Particularly when we look at the statements in the *Book of Mormon* which condemn secret societies and his own words which stated:

> *"We further caution our brethren against the impropriety of the organization of bands or companies, by covenants, oaths, penalties, or secrecies.... pure friendship, always becomes weakened, the very moment you undertake to make it stronger by penal oaths and secrecy."*[42]

Conclusion

There is no doubt that the ritual of the two organisations, whatever guise they may be presented under, derive from the same source. An argument put forward based on coincidence, or even fluke, would quickly flounder. We are therefore faced with one specific question: Did Joseph Smith receive details of the Endowment ceremony prior to becoming a Freemason?

We can take it as a point of evidence, that members of his immediate family and associates who helped him form the church, as well as many close friends, were Craft members. Therefore, membership in such an organisation would not be alien to him. Likewise, the Masonic exposures which were popular at the time were available and freely gave explicit details of ritual. William Morgan supposedly orchestrated the publication of such an exposé in 1826, at Batavia, Genesee County, New York. The Smith family home at this time was in Palmyra, Ontario County, New York.

We then have the suggestion by Smith that Masonic ritual was, in fact, Solomonic in its origins. This was the impression many 18th century Masonic writers gave and in an age of great inquiry, but which lacked sophistication, adherents to the Craft would have honestly believed that it had such antiquity. Therefore, based on what knowledge was available at the time, this assumption was both fair and acceptable.

Any impressionable person, in the mid-19th century, would have been greatly impressed by the pass-grips, pass-words and signs. The addition, or explanation, of the Hiramic legends portrayed, as based upon the biblical story of the dramatic erection of the first house dedicated to the Lord, only gave added authority. Whereas in reality this was no more than an idyllic fable introduced into Masonic ritual to emphasise the salient points of its discipline.

Therefore, if we accept that our ritual cannot boast such antiquity, and that it was formulated late in the 18th century, then Joseph Smith could not have received such revelation from God concerning these man-made Masonic ceremonies, which were definitely not Solomonic in origin. If however, we do accept that the revelation received by Joseph Smith was true and correct, then Freemasonry can indeed boast a great antiquity, truly descended from the first house of the Lord and an unbroken chain of three thousand years.

References / sources

1) McGavin, E. Cecil, *Mormonism and Masonry*, p1

2) Kelly & Hoffman, *Holy Murder*, p79

3) Joseph Smith was the first Prophet, Seer, Revelator and founder of the Church of Jesus Christ of Latter-Day Saints. Extracts from the history of Joseph Smith can be found in the fourth standard work of the church, the Pearl of Great Price, p46.

4) The Endowment ceremony is a story based tableaux structured on the creation of the world, the fall of man, his expulsion from the Garden of Eden, a sequence of instructional ceremonies giving the recipient a series of grips, signs and penalties all predicated upon the adherence of covenants made during each phase, and the subsequent returning to the presence of the Lord. On the completion of the receiving of the signs, token and words, the 'endowed' person is presented to the veil, whereupon his knowledge is tested before he can pass. At the veil, an embrace is held in the form of the "five points of fellowship" while a series of questions and answers are exchanged culminating in a new name being received by the recipient. This is the name by which they will be called to arise on the morning of the first resurrection. Having completed this test, the person is then re-admitted to the presence of the Lord.

5) Beadle, J. H., *The Mysteries of Mormonism*, p409

6) *Ibid.*, p308

7) McGavin, E. Cecil, *Mormonism and Masonry*, p5

8) The Reorganised Church of Jesus Christ of Latter-day Saints was set up after the martyrdom of Joseph Smith. It was at this time when some of the family and followers of

Joseph Smith felt the leadership of the church should fall upon the blood-line of Joseph Smith and not upon Brigham Young.

9) Garments are articles of underclothing worn by the Mormon faithful who have undergone the Endowment (see note 4) ceremony and made certain covenants within those ceremonies. In Freemasonry, they are not unlike the clothing worn by that of the Entered Apprentice at his Initiation. This particular practice however, now having ceased in most modern-day Lodges.

10) Calvin-Rich, H., *Some Differences in Faith*, p31

11) LaRue, C. A., *The Foundations of Masonry*, p101

12) Arbaugh, G. B., *Revelation in Mormonism*, p159

13) Tullidge, E. W., *Life of Joseph the Prophet*, p391

14) Gould, R. K., *The History of Freemasonry*, Vol. II, p279

"Unfortunately, the minutes of Grand Lodge only commence on 24 June 1723. For the history, thereof, of the first six years of the new regime, we are mainly dependent on the account given by Dr Anderson in the Constitutions of 1738, nothing whatever relating to the proceedings of the Grand Lodge, except the 'General Regulations' of 1721, having been inserted in the earlier edition on 1723. From this source I derive the following narrative, in which are preserved as nearly as possible with both the orthographical and the typographical peculiarities of the original:

"King George I. enter'd London most magnificently on 20 September 1714. And after the rebellion was over AD1716, a few Lodges at London finding themselves neglected by Sir Christopher Wren, thought fit to cement under a Grand Master as the centre of Union and Harmony, viz., the Lodges that met,

1. At the Goose and Gridiron Ale-house in St Paul's Church-Yard.

2. At the Crown Ale-house in Parker's Lane near Drury Lane.

3. At the Apple-Tree Tavern in Charles Street, Covent Garden.

4. At the Rumner and Grapes Tavern in Channel Row, Westminster.

They and some old brothers met at the said Apple Tree Tavern, and having put into the chair the oldest Master Mason (now the Master of a Lodge), they constituted themselves a Grand Lodge pro tempore in Due form, and forthwith revived the Quarterly Communication of the Officers of Lodge (called Grand Lodge) resolved to hold the Annual Assembly and Feast, and then to chose a Grand Master from among themselves till they should have the Honour of a Noble Brother at their Head.

On St John Baptist's Day, in the 3rd year of King George I., AD1717, the Assembly and Feast of the Free and Accepted Masons was held at the foresaid Goose and Gridiron Ale-house."

15) *Doctrine and Covenants* (being the third standard work of the Mormon Church), Section 20, p30:

"The rise of the Church of Christ in these last days, being one thousand eight hundred and thirty since the coming of our Lord and Saviour in the flesh, it being regularly organised and established agreeable to the laws of our country, by the will and commandments of God, in the fourth month, and on the sixth day of the month which is called April."

16) Hogan, Mervin. B., *Utah Masons Among The Mormons*, p2

17) *Ibid.,* p2

18) McGavin, E. Cecil, *Mormonism and Masonry*, p13

19) Oliver, Rev George., *The Historical Landmarks of Freemasonry*, p101

20) Wright, Robert C., *Indian Masonry*, p5

21) *Doctrine and Covenants*, Section 24, introductory notes:
".....Harmony, Pennsylvania, July 1830. Though less than four months had elapsed since the Church was organised, persecution had become intense, and the leaders had to seek safety in partial seclusion."

22) *Ibid.*, Section 98, introductory notes:
".....Kirtland, Ohio, August 6, 1833. Patience in persecution enjoined......"

23) *Ibid.*, Section 105, introductory notes:
".....Fishing River, Missouri, June 22, 1834. Mob violence against the Saints in Missouri had increased; and organised bodies from several counties had declared their intent to destroy the people."

24) *Ibid.*, Section 127, introductory notes:
".....Nauvoo, Illinois......September 1, 1842. Because of intense persecution and consequent interference with his labors, the Prophet purposes to go into retirement for a short period."

25) Hogan, Mervin. B., *Utah Masons Among The Mormons*, p3

26) McGavin, E.Cecil, *Mormonism and Masonry*, p13

27) Montgomery, K. H., *Mormons, Masonry and the Morgan Affair*, p1-2
"In 1826, estranged Freemason William Morgan published an exposé of the Masonic Order in New York. On September 11 of the same year he was arrested for petty theft. The following day he was released and escorted against his will by several men to Fort Niagara on the Canadian Frontier and was held until September 19. From there he disappeared never to be seen again, but the results of his disappearance had a disastrous effect on the Craft. It was been alleged by many that he was murdered by Freemasons and subsequently in 1828 the Anti-Masonic political party was created and sponsored candidates in the 1832 and 1836 Presidential elections. The effect on the Craft was to reduce the 227 Lodges of New York in 1827 to only 41 by 1835."

28) Meré, Mario., *The Morgan Affair*, p1

29) Hogan, Mervin. B., *Utah Masons Among The Mormons*, p4

30) Montgomery, K.H., *Mormons, Masonry and the Morgan Affair*, p3

31) Hogan, Mervin B., *Utah Masons Among The Mormons*,

32) Montgomery, K. H., *Mormons, Masonry and the Morgan Affair*, p3

33) *Doctrine and Covernants*, Section 124:28, 39-42

34) *Minutes, General Conference of the Church*, Nauvoo, Illinois, 3 October 1841

35) *History of the Church*, Vol 4, p449

36) *Millenial Star*, Vol 5, p104

37) *Emulation Ritual*, Explantion of the Second Degree Tracing Board.

38) *The Return*, Vol 2,

39) McGavin, E. Cecil, *Mormonism and Masonry*, p199

40) *Ibid.*, p192-194

41) Whalen, William J., *The Latter-Day Saints in the Modern Day World*, p203-4
42) *Times and Seasons*, vol. 1, p133.

*How the chance discovery of twenty-nine insignificant words
validated and confirmed early 18th century ritual practices*

Those Twenty-Nine Words

(Written in 2005)

To many Freemasons, it seems ritual is the most important part of the Craft, after all, we lean it by rote, we deliver it as skilfully as possible and sadly, we judge each exponent on the capacity of his delivery. We also absolve ourselves from our poor ritual delivery by claiming that it is archaic, repetitive and boring. We then follow that up with the claim that our new Initiates leave because of it and then we argue that it causes the meetings to go on to long.

It is almost an indictment of our society that to date, we have no formal training programme on how to deliver ritual, that job being left to the Director of Ceremonies which in the many cases I have seen, his concern is more about perambulations, than teaching ritual. Sadly, in all our years, we have not found a medium of learning that would make all men equal in the exchange of our catechetical instruction and all the time we carry on in this manner, good men will forsake the opportunity of attaining Freemasons highest honour, the Chair of King Solomon, because of their fear or capacity to learn the ritual.

But this paper is not about ritual delivery, it does not introduce a finite training programme, nor does it offer any solutions to our learning problems. It does however examine the point of how important our ritual is, it takes a closer look at its origins, its errors and mistakes and hopefully it may just awaken some to the beauty of its contents, give an insight in to its actual meaning and encourage some to look at our ritual in a new light of appreciation rather than the burden we all have to bear on our way to the Chair.

Ritual, by our own understanding, is an established form of practice, observance or ceremony carried out in a solemn and respectful manner. We often associate it with religious liturgy or formal occasions, but because our practices are a consistent form of ceremony, we can call it ritual as opposed to a rite, which is religious liturgy. Our ritual has not been composed or invented, but rather is a perpetuation of the activities, practices, customs and usages of the daily work of the Cathedral builder and his Lodge, and has only ever been modified to help us understand, to include or to highlight a salient point of our discipline. So, the ritual actually becomes the work of each Lodge and that is why ritual is the centre of Freemasonry. Believe it or not, without such work Freemasonry would be bland, uninteresting and insipid.

I am always so excited that at the culmination of our work, the Worshipful Master looks at the Senior Warden and exclaims: "...the labours of the evening being ended, you have my command to close the Lodge." And with three distinct knocks of the gavel, he acknowledges the completion of our labours to his satisfaction and the Brethren adjourn for refreshment as a reward for their labours.

Not many of us realise, but it was almost certainly Civil Law that inadvertently started the whole process of ritual when it demanded that all members of an Incorporated or Chartered body, whether a Company or Fraternity, be required to take an Oath or Obligation. Civil Law also required that each professional trade have an official Charter to operate. Applications for Charters would have to include rules, aims and objectives of the trade and this was to ensure quality as well as helping to maintain standards of work.

We know that Companies or Fraternities held assemblies and surviving building records do seem to indicate that not only was there some kind of organisation, but that the organisation covered a much larger area which seems directly opposed to the town based organisation Mysteries. We certainly find records of the minstrels, who like the itinerant Masons, had to wander about the country to find work, and were subject to wide territorial jurisdictions. John of Gaunt established a court at Tutbury in 1381 to enact laws for minstrels and to determine controversies affecting them which covered five neighbouring counties. Therefore, it is not implausible to consider that Masons may have had a similar system and that is what the Regius MS seems to indicate. The Cook MS also refers to annual or triennial congregations of Masters and Fellows which was said to have been established by Athelstan. That Stone workers and Freemasons had customs is not in doubt, as we find in the building accounts of Sandgate Castle in 1539, a "jurat" or member of a municipal body was paid his expenses while riding to communicate with the Controller or Master of the Works "...

concerning the use and customs of Freemasons and hewers…"

At these places where they met, they would have their Charter to ensure their meeting was lawful and recognised, they would also have copies of the rules and limits or Charges as we know them, of their operation. It is obvious that they would discuss issues of the day, working practices, disciplinary procedures and receive Apprentices. On large sites like the building of a Cathedral, the established work force of Masons would have used a Lodge. Hence, we read in the Vale Royal Abbey building accounts of 1278, carpenters were paid to erect Lodges. The same goes for Mason's Lodges and workshops at Catterick Bridge in 1421, Kirby Muxloe Castle in 1481 and so on. Then we have details of repairs to Mason's Lodges at Beaumaris Castle in 1330 and Westminster Abbey in 1413. In both England and Scotland, we find references to Lodges at York, in 1352, which refers to by-laws and ordinances. In Canterbury, in 1429, which refers to its members as the "Masons of the Lodge". In Aberdeen, in 1481, which refers to conditions of employment. In Edinburgh, in 1491, which refers to written statements of old established customs.

They had a Scrivener to keep records, a Treasurer to account for monies and make payments, a Master of the Fabric or Clerk of the Works to oversee the building, an Almoner to care for the injured and distressed and a Chaplain for pastoral matters. They would also have contributed to a box, for the relief of injured members and a Patron Saint whose day they would take as a holiday to go in procession to the Church.

These are a few simplistic explanations that give us a small picture of the early Lodge situation and it is from these conditions that our work emanated in the form of elaborations of existing practices or innovations that made the usage more appropriate to a Speculative Mason rather than an Operative Mason. For example: The Charges of a Mason as found in the *Old MS Constitutions* were adapted for the Speculative Mason, however in this process of adaptation, very little was lost as the spirit of moral behaviour that was expected of our Operative brother shines through as clear as day to the Speculative Mason.

We learn from the *Old MS Constitutions* that there was always an opening prayer or invocation to start the proceedings, this was followed by the legendary history of the Craft, the Charges regarding his expected behaviour were then read and the Apprentice then took his Obligation or swore an Oath of fidelity to keep his trade business and skills secret. The meeting or ceremony was then ended with a closing prayer of benediction.

However, later Scottish documents dated from about 1696, contain catechetical exchanges, spiritual practices and the Five Points of Fellowship. But the late Masonic Scholar Bro Harry Carr, explains that the Masonic student will have difficulty in accepting these later documents as accurate, for the central theme is one of secrecy which has an Oath attached and any such record or written revelation would actually be a breach of that Oath and therefore we should consider the records suspect in their content. Therefore, despite their interesting and fascinating nature, they cannot be used as evidence and their validity challenged unless there was a way they could be proved authentic.

Surprisingly, this is not as easy as it may sound for these old manuscripts do find their way back into the Masonic fold, but this is by more luck than judgement as they are not held by Lodges, but generally filed away in book, ledgers or trunks in dusty old store rooms or other collections, the owner being none the wiser of their existence, their Masonic association of in fact, their value.

Then we had the problem that faced Masons in 1718, when the new Grand Master, George Payne, who was obviously aware of the existence of these old records, asked Lodges that possessed any records concerning the Craft that they be brought to Grand Lodge. Unfortunately, this simple request met with disastrous results as many scrupulous brethren, fearing the papers might fall into strange hands, burnt then rather than follow the request. Sadly, in this one simple misguided act, these faithful and honest brethren who had the principles of fidelity imprinted on their hearts, stood firm and done their duty and in the process may have wiped out precious historical records, rituals and other information regarding the practice of Freemasonry in the Westminster area during the 16th century. However, records tell us that at least six documents did survive the cull and reached Grand Lodge.

One thing is for sure, whatever Grand Master Payne or Grand Lodge learned from the gathering of the documents is not known for there is no further record, however it is fair to say that when the Grand Master Duke of Montagu "...finding fault with all the copies of the Old Gothic Constitutions, order'd Brother James Anderson A.M. to digest the same in a new and better method..." he did exactly that and used them as a basis for his Constitutions of 1723 and 1738.

Having studied this situation as carefully as possible, at this stage I am not convinced that any great information was destroyed or lost as just a decade later we find the publication of Pritchard's *Masonry Dissected*, an exposure of 1730, which contained all of the known ritual used at that time. Its authenticity was never challenged and such was the turmoil caused by the exposure with irregular Masons gaining entrance to regular Lodges, the Grand Lodge response almost validated the exposure because it chose to reverse the passwords of the First and Secord Degrees, rather than deny the publication outright.

To return to pre-1717 ritual, the main foundation of early ritual in England is based on a group of three Scottish documents dated between 1696 and 1714, written out laboriously by hand and possibly used as a guide or aides-memoir. They are:

- *The Edinburgh Register House* MS, dated 1696 – Found in 1930, in the Old Register House, Edinburgh, among a number of papers transferred there in 1808 and was in no way related to any of the papers or records which it was stored with.
- *The Chetwode Crawley* MS, dated *c*.1700 – Found in a collection of volumes purchased as a lot, *c*.1900, from a second-hand book collector.
- *The Kevan* MS, dated *c*.1714 – Found in 1954, among a collection of old legal documents belonging to a firm of Solicitors practising in Berwickshire.

Unlike the more formal and printed *Masonry Dissected*, these made no outlandish claims about what they were or what they contained, they were not written for profit, nor out of spite, and there is no reason to doubt the respectability of their origins. But however interesting the MS might be, as previously explained, any such ritual presented as secrecy being the main theme is already in breach of the very Oath to which it pertains and without any specific link to any Lodge, they must forever remain under suspicion as without the validation of such documents, they can only be seen as interesting or curious artefacts of a bygone age. But by a very rare stroke of luck, an interesting discovery led students to the possibility of validating the previously three mentioned documents.

Haughfoot, was a hamlet near Stow, Galashiels, in the Scottish Lowlands and at the end of the 17th century, it consisted mainly of a staging post for horses and carriages, and would have been the most unlikely place for a Lodge to be established as the region consisted mainly of gentry and local land owners, not stone works or masons. But it was in fact, the place where Scotland's first wholly non-operative Lodge was founded, on 22 December 1702 and here's the twist of fate, it would appear that at the commencement of that Lodge, the ceremonies were written in the first several pages of the Lodge minute book to the extent that the last 29 words of the ceremony commenced at the top of a new page and at the completion of the written ritual text we find the following words:

"The same day"

Indicating that the ritual text was completed and the first meeting of the Lodge were held on the same day.

At a later date, a new recorder or secretary would have noticed the ritual text in the book and believing it to be a breach of the Oath of secrecy of the Order, removed all but the last 29 words which you recall commenced on a new page where were also recorded the first minutes of the new Lodge. Those remaining words were actually the finale of the admission procedure of the Master Mason or Fellow Craft under the Scottish two-degree system practised at that time and on inspection, these words, known as the *Haughfoot Fragment*, were very similar to the three aforementioned ritual documents, in particular *The Edinburgh Register House* MS. Thus, this fragment provided that all important link to a working Lodge which in turn provided a starting point or basis to a standard ritual text used in Scotland between 1696 and *c.*1714, and possible up to 50 or even 100 years before that.

At this point I am sure you are wondering exactly what the 29 words, well on their own they seem quite insignificant but here they are:

> *"...of entrie as the apprentice did Leaving out (The Common Judge) Then they whisper the word as before – and the Master Mason grips his hand after the ordinary way."*

However, when compare with the *The Edinburgh Register House* MS, there are quite striking and unmistakable similarities:

> *"...of entrie as the apprentice did only leaving out the common judge then the masons whisper the word among themselves beginning at the youngest as formerly.... Then the master gives him the word and gripes his hand after the masons way..."*

This discovery proved the first real link with Lodge ritual practices and subsequent to this, a whole range of other documents, both English, Irish and Scottish, opened the way for a new study of the development of our ritual. The late Bro Harry Carr, being himself an expert in early ritual development, raises an important point. In the introduction of his work, *Early French Exposures* he says,

> *"One important point needs to be stressed. It is a matter of pure coincidence that the earliest group of "Ritual" documents are all of Scottish origin and, at best, they can only be taken as representing Scottish practice. But when later texts begin to make their appearance including those of English origin, it becomes evident that despite various differences representing separate streams of development, there was a kind of nucleus of basic elements that was common to the practice of both countries."*

Surprisingly, although we have this wonderful collection of texts, neatly woven together to demonstrate the development of early ritual, we have had to be reliant on exposures in England to demonstrate the evolution of the tri-gradal or three-degree system.

Firstly, we have no record of the term "Degree" being used until 1730, with the publication of Pritchard's *Masonry Dissected*, but we cannot assume this was the first time the term was used, but we can be sure that a third part of the system was in use. As early as 1725, we have a set of minutes from *The Society of Lovers of Music and Architecture* (*Philo Musicae et Architecturae Societas)*, not a Lodge as one would expect, but rather a club for society gentlemen in London. Founded in February 1725, they met at the Queens Head Tavern, Temple Bar, London and were a society set up exclusively for Freemasons and if a prospective member was not a Freemason, then they would simple Initiate them before receiving them into their society. Hence we read from their minutes of the 12 May 1725, Mr Charles Cotton, who was made a Mason on 24 December 1724 and a Fellow Craft on 18 February 1725 at another Lodge, was "Passed a Master" during a meeting of the society. And that unusual record are the first details of the first conferment of what we now know as being the Third degree.

But the full content of the Third Degree was not known until the aforementioned *Masonry Dissected*, where we read for the first time, details of the Hiramic legend. However, this was not the first time we read loss and recovery theme. Four years earlier, we read in the *Graham* MS, the story of the death of Noah, and how his sons, Shem, Ham and Japheth went to their father's body to discover a secret that he had taken with him to the grave. Here is a reprint of the story in loose written in modern English.

"We have it by tradition and still some reference to scripture that caused Shem, Ham and Japheth to go to their father Noah's grave to try to see if they could find anything about him to lead them to the veritable secret which this famous preacher had concerning all things that were necessary for them for the new world.

Now these three men had already agreed that if they did not find the very thing itself, then the first thing that they found was to be to them, a secret. They not doubting, but did most firmly believe that God was able and would also prove willing through their faith prayer and obedience for to cause what they did find for to prove as veritable to them as if they had received the secret at first from God himself.

So came they to the grave and finding nothing save the dead body all most consumed away, they took a grip at a finger, it came away from joint to joint, so to the elbow, they reared up the dead body and supported it setting foot to foot, knee to knee, breast to breast, cheek to check and hand to back and cried out help us Father, as if they had said their Father in Heaven, help us now for our earthly father cannot. They then laid down the dead body again. Not knowing what to do, one said here is yet marrow in this bone and the second said, but a dry bone and the third said it stinketh, so they agreed for to give it a name as is known to Freemasonry to this day."

A rather intriguing story which demonstrates the loss, recovery and fidelity theme which has become such a predominant part of our ritual. This also confuses many exponents of the Royal Ark Mariners Degree who have at times wrongly claimed that their Order was founded or derived from this story.

So there it is, a brief look at how some of our ritual was discovered, validated and exposed, but it was not until the Act of Union of 1813 and the work of the Lodges of Reconciliation and Promulgation, did Freemasonry really get its act together and formalise and regulate the kind of ritual that you and I enjoy today.

Before I close, I thought it might just be interesting to know that despite the work of Grand Lodge and other bodies that have promoted their specific ritual, i.e. Emulation, Taylors, West End and Logic to name just a few, it is still full of errors, grammatical mistakes and historical inaccuracies. But as Freemasons we are forgiving, for we all accept that ritual is not the gospel truth, but rather a series of exchanges and lectures, prepared, learnt and delivered for our personal improvement and development.

So much of its content has been copied or taken from earlier or contemporary sources and here a few examples:

On the night of our Initiation we are told, as part of the ceremony which culminates in the Charge, that we owe certain duties to our neighbour by acting with him on the square and by doing to him in similar cases what you would wish he would do to you. Compare that with the words of Mencius, a contemporary of Confucius, who wrote the following in about 300 BC.

> *"A Master Mason, in teaching his apprentices, makes use of the compasses and the square. Ye who are engaged in the pursuit of wisdom must also use the compasses and the square. A man should abstain from doing unto others what he would not they should do to him. This is called the principle of acting on the square."*

In the Second Degree we are told how *Seven* makes a Lodge perfect, *Seven* has an allusion to the seven Liberal Arts and Sciences and that King Solomon's Temple was seven years and upwards in building, completing and dedicating. Well it's the latter part of this sentence that interests us at this point and takes us into the realms of the re-building of London after the Great Fire of 1666. The Government of the day prepared three new statutes for the re-building of London and one particular statute, took steps to increase the supply of labour, by suspending all local trade and encouraging an influx of workmen from outside London. My point being in writing that statue they used the phrase, "for seven years and upwards" indicating the minimum length of time it would take to rebuild the city.

Our ritual authors were obviously very well read and although what seems archaic phraseology now, was in fact contemporary language of the day. For example, phrases like, "the great luminary" "labour and refreshment" and "darkness visible", are all used in Milton's *Paradise Lost*.

While "balm of consolation" was used in Bronte's *Pride and Prejudice*, and "evasion, equivocation or mental reservation" occurs in a declaration incorporated in the 1678, Act of Parliament concerning the Coronation Oath.

"Fortunes Wheel" refers to the Roman Goddess Fortuna and is found no less than five times in the works of Shakespeare alone, and "being of good report" "the emblematical Lights" "the four cardinal virtues" and "that bright morning star" can all be found in various editions of the Bible.

Of course, here are just a few examples of the terms and phrases that we use at each of our meetings that are found in our contemporary classics, but what is more the point, what those ritual writers could not find, they invented and tagged it on to an existing event to give it some credence. Here are a few examples:

True or false? There was a certain Assistant High Priest named Jachin, who, so our ritual informs us, officiated at the dedication of King Solomon's Temple and it appears, was so respected, that the right-hand pillar at the porch way or entrance to the Temple was named after him.

False. He did not assist at the dedication of the Temple, and the Pillar was not named after him. According to the Bible, neither the High Priest or his Assistant played any part in the dedication which was presided over by Solomon, who we are told spoke and prayed. The Bible gives us the name Jachin, meaning "He (God) will establish", therefore neither the Pillar or its name have anything to do with the unknown alleged, Assistant High Priest, Jachin.

True or false? Those two pillars that adorned the porch way or entrance to the Temple were formed hollow so as to serve as archives to Freemasonry for therein were deposited the constitutional rolls.

False. Factually speaking, there is absolutely no evidence to suggest that Freemasonry existed in those days, or constitutional rolls regarding Freemasonry written.

True or false? Our ritual tells us that, "Those Pillars were further adorned with two spherical balls on which were delineated maps of the celestial and terrestrial globes, pointing out Masonry Universal."

False. There are three problems with this statement, firstly the Volume of Sacred Law explains that the "spherical balls" were in fact "bowls". The second issue is that at that time, the terrestrial world was yet to be discovered or delineated in map form. The third point is that Masonry at that time was not universal and did not exist.

True or false. "For God said in strength will I establish mine house to stand firm forever."

False. In Masonic teaching, we learn we learn that the import of the names for the pillars were, "In Strength" and "To Establish" respectively. This conforms to the writings of Flavius Josephus who wrote in the 1st century AD that Boaz means "In Him Strength or In It Strength" and Jachin means "He Will establish or It will establish" (Antiquities of the Jews). Masonic teaching also advises us that when conjoined, the words mean "Stability", for God said, "In strength I will establish this mine house to stand firm for ever". However, nowhere in any version of the Bible do we read God using these words. The nearest we can get to the phrase is found in 1 Chronicles, 17:12 which says: "He shall build me an house, and I will establish his throne for ever."

True or False? The builders went to receive their wages in the Middle Chamber of King Solomon's Temple and their ascent was opposed by the Junior Warden, who demanded a password and pass grip.

False. It must have been an immense chamber to store the wages, corn, wine and oil for some 180,000 builders to have their ascent opposed by the Junior Warden, whose hand may well have withered after receiving the token from so many.

These are but a few of the amusing common errors that abound in our ritual, but I have repeatedly observed that the purpose of the ritual is to highlight salient points of our discipline and to encourage us to reflect on our own personal behaviour, it is not a lesson in history or grammar. Our story tells us that Hiram Abiff, was murdered because of his unshakable fidelity and that Brethren, is the lesson we learn from the building, completing and dedicating of King Solomon's Temple. It had to be dramatic. It had to have impact on us personally. It had to impress upon our minds that we that we must die rather than reveal our secrets, or suffer a horrible death, as a result of the punishments attached to any unlawful disclosure. As secrecy is the complete thread of Freemasonry, then such are the threats we observe.

Having made several comments on ritual, I cannot allow this paper to close without adding my own personal view on the subject.

Firstly, it is important to resist any change that may attempt to modernise our ritual, it is what it is. Unless one could conceive any unshakable argument as to why it should be changed, we should leave it exactly as it is, confident in the knowledge that what we have been entrusted with, under our stewardship, can be passed on to the next generation, untouched.

Secondly, it is incumbent upon all of us to ensure that each new Initiate understands that he will be expected to progress through each Office, culminating in the honour of being placed in the Chair of King Solomon and that on the way he will be expected to learn, within the realm of his capacity, every part of the ritual. This should be raised with him at his interview that he may understand the part he will play in the permanency of Freemasonry and its attendant usages, practices and customs.

Thirdly, it is a fact that many Brethren choose to learn more about this noble science than what is contained within the pages of our ritual books. In reality, it means that we have many Brethren skilled in the art of delivery, but little knowledge of anything else. If we could just extend the general Masonic knowledge of Brethren, then a deeper appreciation of what we are actually doing will be developed.

My last gripe is directed against two types of selfish Brethren, the first are those that find it necessary to prompt an unsuspecting Brother during his ritual delivery which is so wrong. It is rude, it is embarrassing and it undermines the role of the Director of Ceremonies and it has no place in today's Lodge. The second are those, that through the lack of effort they put in, in learning their words, actually have the audacity to try and bluster their way through a ceremony. The fact is, it is obvious to all those present, which Brethren have actually put the time in to learning and those that have not. Therefore, please, at the very least, be honest with yourself and if you are not prepared to make the effort, then do not accept the assignment as, it does you, the Lodge, its members, the guests and visitors and the Candidate, no favours whatsoever.

*Examining the history given to Freemasonry in both the 1723 and
1738 Books of Constitution and how this misled many eminent
Masonic scholars and historians to arrive at some of the more
preposterous theories and associations of Speculative
Freemasonry*

Surviving History

(Written in 2008)

It was on the 24 June 1717, at the Goose and Gridiron, near St. Paul's Yard, London, that the first assembly of the Grand Lodge of England met. Unfortunately, the minutes of Grand Lodge only commence on 24 June 1723 and as for our history, we are mainly dependent on a retrospective account given by Dr James Anderson in the Constitutions of 1738.

Having made that statement, we should never be in any doubt that Speculative Freemasonry had been practiced in England for at least 100 years prior to that date, although not necessarily with any regularity, but certainly in some form. Thus throughout that period, 1620–1717, we find many references to Freemasonry or the like. For example:

In 1620, the records of the Company of Masons show us that they had a policy of receiving Accepted members. In that year, John Hince, Evan Lloyd and James Ffrench, were admitted by Acception into some sort of inner-circle of Masons or fellowship. Records further show us that they had been apprentices and members of the Company and on the payment of a gratuity were received into the special group. These types of groups are generally considered by historians to be made up purely of Accepted Masons. The problem is however that there are no records to show if this was a regular meeting within the Masons Company. It may be worth reminding ourselves at this state the many Guilds and Companies accepted men, not engaged in their particular trade, as patrons or a means of bestowing an honour or special privilege and they included on their rolls most of the wealthy men of the nation. Royal patronage was also common, Edward Ill, Henry IV, Henry VI and Henry VIII, were all Guild members.

It was in 1646, that the Antiquarian Elias Ashmole, entered those immortal words in his diary claiming:

"I was made a Free Mason at Warrington in Lancashire."

In attendance that evening were only seven other Lodge members, none of which had anything to do with the builders or masons profession, but were country gentlemen. In his Diary, Ashmole makes special mention of one *"Richard Penket, Warden"*, which is enough evidence to show us that this was an old Operative Lodge which was in the process or receiving Accepted Speculative Masons. How do we know this? Because in early Lodges, the members elected a Warden to rule over them and not a Master.

A chance discovery of a piece of scrap paper dated by the British Museum at about 1650 proved to be another piece of evidence. Randall Holme, a contemporary of Ashmole and author of a 1688 publication entitled *An Accademie of Armory*, in which he stated:

> *"I cannot but honour the fellowship of the Masons because of its antiquity, and the more as being myself a member of that society of Freemasons."*

The scrap of paper that was found is now known as the *Harlean fragment* and is the first known allusion to Masonic words and signs and says the following:

> *"There is several words and signs of a free mason to be revealed to you which... you keep secret and not to reveal the same to any...person but to the masters and fellows of the said Society of Free Masons..."*

Also found among his papers were a list of 27 names believed to be the members of a Lodge at Chester, each of whom paid a fee *"for to be a free mason."* Randall Holmes name is 14th on that list. Of those 27 names only six were Masons by trade.

Published in 1672, Marvell's *Rehearsal Transprosed,* contains the first reference on English Soil, relating to the Masons Word (Masonic words and the Masons Word are distinctly different) and it says:

> '... *and as those that have the masons word secretly discern one another;...".*

In 1676, we find the following satirical paragraph in a weekly sheet published in London and known as *"Poor Robin's Intelligence"*:

> '...*to give notice, that the Modern Green-ribbon's Cabal!, together with the Ancient Brother-hood of the Rosy-Cross; the Hermetick Adepti, and the Company of Accepted Masons,*

*intend all to Dine together on the 31 November next, at the
Flying-Bull in Windmill-Mill-Crown Street; having already
given order for great store of Black-Swam Pies, Poach'd
Phoenixes Eggs, Haunches of Unicorns, &c. To be provided on
that occasion; All idle people that can spare so much time from
the Coffee-house, may repair thither to be spectators of the
Solemnity: But are advised to provide themselves Spectacles of
Malleable Glass; For otherwise 'tis thought the said Societies
will (as hitherto) make their Appearance Invisible."*

In 1682, we find the next reference from the diary of Elias Ashmole relating
to Freemasonry which was made some 36 years later, he writes:
*"I received a summons to appear at a Lodge to be held next
day at Masons Hall London."*

His entry tells us that he saw six men received into Freemasonry, four of
those being members of the Company of Masons and two were not. There
were eight Lodge members present. In fact out of the total of the 14 names
present it would appear that:
- Eight were members of the London Company of Masons.
- Seven of them were part of the Livery of the Company.
- Four of the Seven were part of the Court of Assistants of
  the Company.
- Three were well known contractors whose names would be
  found in the building of St Paul's Cathedral.
- One was a chief importer of stone into London during that
  period.

Plot's *Natural History of Staffordshire* of 1686 includes a summary of the
legendary history of Masonry, obviously based on a version of the *old
manuscript constitutions,* and a description of Accepted masonry. He also
classifies two types of Mason. The first is obviously an operative Mason
bound by the *"manners and charges"* and the second it would appear that
they are or have been *"sworn after their fashion".* Plot also talks about the
"Custom", as he calls it, being *"...spread more or less over the Nation."*
along with *"...certain secret signs...".*

In 1698, one M. Winter, issued the following warning to this "Christian
Generation" and declared:

"Having thought it needful to warn you of the mischief's and evils practiced in the sight of God by those called Freed Masons, I say take care lest their ceremonies and secret swearings take hold of you..."

The *Tatler* in 1709, refers to another organisation which had;
"... signes and tokens like Freemasons".

So to recap on the first section of this lecture, we can confirm that prior to 1717, Masonry or Speculative Freemasonry in some form was practiced, not necessarily with any regularity by:
- The Company of Masons in 1620 and 1682
- The Company of Accepted Masons in 1676
- The Society of Free Masons in 1686 and 1688
- The Fellowship of Masons in 1688
- The Freed Masons in 1698

And that:
- In 1620, men were admitted by Acception to the Company of Masons
- In 1646 Elias Ashmole was "made a Mason" at a ceremony attended only by country gentlemen
- In 1650 the Society of Freemasons used "words and signs"
- In 1672, there was a Mason Word
- In 1686 there were two types of Mason, the first an operative mason bound by the *"manners and charges"* and the second it would appear are *"sworn after their fashion"*
- Again in 1686 we find Accepted Masonry *"spread more or less over the Nation"* and that they had *"certain use secret signs"*
- In 1698 they had ceremonies and secret swearings
- In 1709 Freemasons used signs and tokens.

We can therefore safely assume that from 1620–1717 Freemasonry or what could be classed as a type of Freemasonry, was active and was spread throughout the land.

However by 1707, Edwin Strong Snr who alludes to the fact that he laid the last stone on the dome of St Paul's Cathedral, tells us that:

"Yet still in the South, the Lodges were more and more disused, partly by the neglect of the Masters and Wardens and partly by not having a Noble Grand Master in London, and the annual assembly was not duly attended..."

And likewise the 1738 *Book of Constitutions* tells that:
"King George I, entered London most magnificently on 20 September 1714. And after the rebellion was over AD1716, a few Lodges at London finding themselves neglected..."

So by the early part of the 18th century Lodges were more and more disused, mainly by neglect and it is at this point I want you to hold that last thought while we progress to the next section of the lecture.

One of the most notable pleasures of the 17th century, so history informs us, was the Coffee House and the Tavern. These places of social gatherings quickly began to attain a significant degree of political importance from the volume of talk which they caused. Each sect, party or even fashion had its favourite meeting place and London life in general, grew more animated by their presence. It was the establishment of such meeting places that no doubt set the scene for many a club or convivial society to be formed. Thus we find in London such societies springing up with the most exotic names one can imagine:

- The Most Ancient, Honourable and Venerable Society of Adams
- The Loyal and Friendly Society of Blue and Orange
- The Ancient and Joyous Order of the Hiccolites
- The Very Honourable Order of Cabalarians

And of course those mentioned earlier:

- The Modern Green-ribbon's Cabal
- The Ancient Brother-hood of the Rosy-Cross
- The Hermetick Adepti

The list, as one can imagine, is quite extensive and all would have had their own joining criteria, rules, practices and in many cases unique initiations as I have already mentioned in 1709, when the *Tatler* referred to another organisation which had:

"signes and tokens like Freemasons"

Against that backdrop, The Ancient Order of Free and Accepted Masons did not seem out of place at all, especially when you examine the membership or club rules these associations had in common which was:

- They met in rooms separate from the main area of the tavern
- They considered all men were equal and *"none need give his place to a Finer man"*.
- Anyone who swore was made to *"forfeit twelve pence"* and the man who began a quarrel *"shall also receive a fine"*.
- *"Maudlin lovers"* were forbidden *"in Corners to mourn"* for all were expected to *"be brisk, and talk, but not too much"*.
- *"Sacred Things"* must be excluded from the conversation, and the patrons could neither *"profane Scripture, nor saucily wrong Affairs of State with an irreverent tongue"*.
- Women were excluded.

Recognise any of those rules? All men are equal, no quarrelling, no discussions about religion or politics, women excluded, it almost sounds like the start of modern day Freemasonry.

Having now made the point that convivial societies and clubs, with their beliefs, practices, initiations and ceremonial were common at the start of the 18th century, I shall now move on to the next section.

The third section of my lecture deals with one Dr James Anderson, a Scottish Presbyterian Minister who was the Chaplain to St Paul's Lodge in 1710. Historians tell us that the St Pauls Lodge was an Operative Lodge attached to the St Paul's Cathedral site. However, in 1715, being guilty of some unknown misdemeanor, Anderson was expelled from the Lodge prior to him being made Master. But not being daunted by what had happened to him, he became associated with Freemasons and helped shape this new and revised club for Gentleman which within a few years would be known as *The Antient Society of Free and Accepted Masons*, and it is this organisation that Grand Lodge recognises today as the starting point of organised or modern day Speculative Freemasonry.

Having only a limited amount of knowledge, it took Anderson several years to help conceive and perfect a system of Speculative Freemasonry that we would possible recognise today with a three degree system, complete with the Hiramic legend to name but two items. Sadly however, he did overlook certain aspects or practices which he appeared not to be aware of at the time and which related in particular to the Holy Royal Arch which was introduced almost retrospectively later that same century. 1717.

But Anderson was a gifted man and within a few years, by stealing their history, he had convinced many that this new club was an extension of the Company of Freemasons formed centuries before, in fact using his influence to help the cause, he managed to have every scrap of paper purporting to be of Masonic origin to be brought to his the Grand Lodge to be examined. The effects as you know were disastrous and many documents were burned rather than be handed over, as such was the fidelity demonstrated by some brethren in those days. However, as most of these documents, were copies of documents relating to Operative practices, they became the tool by which Anderson promoted the antiquity of the new club.

Using, shall we say, a little or rather a lot of poetic license, he added to that history to form the first *Book of Constitutions* in 1723 and by the time the second *Book of Constitutions* was published in 1788, he had secured the history so firmly that the Society of Free and Accepted Masons could now trace its origins back to the building of King Solomon's Temple. Now how clever was that?

But it was the second *Book of Constitutions,* and many of you have heard me say this before, where Anderson gave full reign to his imagination and wrote a full and concise history from Adam right down to the Crafts "so called" revival in 1717. Additionally, any English monarch or historical character that had in any manner patronised architects or masons was listed as a Grand Master or Grand Warden.

And this is where the problems started, for it is from these *Books of Constitutions* that we wrongly derived the notion that the traditions of Freemasons Lodges have existed from ancient times and because Andersons Constitutions were published with the sanction of Grand Lodge, they became sacrosanct, never to be challenged. In fact, so acceptable was this work to become that it continued to be printed with various updates until about 1784. The work was plagiarised by William Preston of the Prestonian lecture fame, whose book *Illustrations of Masonry* had almost a dozen editions and continued to be published after his death in 1861.

The *Book of Constitutions* and Preston's work were exported to North America and translated into German and French, thus giving this misinformation the widest circulation possible, indoctrinating Masonic historians and influencing theories of origin well into the 19th and 20th century. Subsequently, out of that history of Andersons, sprung as many fanciful theories regarding the origin of our Craft as you could imagine, and all untenable. In fact over the years many men of great eminence have tended to develop theories along the most implausible lines and then convince us with the most eloquent and convincing well-written books.

And this concludes the third part of this lecture which was to examine the possibility that Anderson influenced or help form a club or convivial society which in the process of doing so, stole the complete history and legends and some of the practices, initiatory rites and ceremonial known to him from his previous association with the St Paul's Lodge.

This final section deals with the more worrying questions that if something does not have a history, why do we feel we have to create one? And why in these days of great enlightenment do we as a fraternity continue to confuse our Speculative occupation with a whole range of other historic associations? I constantly read books and articles, which endeavor, through wordy speculation and sheer romance, to connect the shape of our modern day rituals with those of ancient civilizations or medieval practices, and I wish I had a pound for every time a brother has asked me what I think of the "Da Vinci Code?" What I say is this; it has absolutely nothing to do with Freemasonry whatsoever.

We must all therefore ask ourselves this question?

> *"Why have we never read or heard of the discovery of a medieval or ancient Speculative Lodge room?"*

Quite simple that is because there are none!

> *"Have we heard of any great medieval manuscript, which allays itself to our present day fraternity?"*

No! Because the Gothic Constitutions were written for the benefit of Operative Masons, not Speculative Freemasons.

We must therefore conclude that history itself has either been very unkind to Speculative Freemasonry or in plain and simple terms, there is no history!

Having said that, we have the *Old* MS, and as I explained earlier we learn from Dr Anderson that between June 1719 and June 1720 several valuable manuscripts concerning the ancient *"regulations, charges, secrets and usages"* were burnt by some scrupulous brethren, *"that those papers might not fall into strange hands"*. However, I think on this point, most historians would concede that they were no more than copies of Old

Operative Charges and although of some value to the Fraternity, it is doubtful that they would have contained any more information than that which already existed in the old MS form, or in fact that was later to been revealed by the 18th century exposures.

We must face the fact that our Tri-gradual degree system, our allegorical associations with Solomon's Temple and the death of its chief Architect were all introduced as allegorical stories based on historical fable and formed into our ritual to illustrate salient points of our discipline and are no more than the fictional and romantic imaginations of our early Masonic leaders. The general consensuses of opinion being that the three degrees were formulated and introduced approximately between 1723 and 1730 and performed in the back rooms of Ale houses, not Lodge rooms. Lodge rooms only came about after the use of Assembly rooms became popular in the late 18th century, likewise, it was the Lodges of Promulgation and Reconciliation, before and after the Act of Union of 1813, that helped, under the direction of Grand Lodge, to continually modify the ritual until the early 19th century when the degrees were formalised as we know them today. In fact, Degrees were not practiced by Operative fraternities; they had grades or classes of Mason.

It is also agreed that the free adaptation of the administrative set up of the London Trade Companies with their Masters, Wardens, Secretaries, Treasurers and Almoners and a two-degree Acception system that was stolen from the Company or Society of Masons, that being the Apprentice and Fellowcrafts, went to make up the first true Speculative Lodges in London. We even know that the Coats of Arms of the Company of Masons was used to promote the cause, which even today is found on the left hand side of the United Grand Lodges logo.

Now to some degree, these old Lodges may have included some Operative Masons, hence the introduction in 1722, of the term Free and Accepted. However, judging by the decline of that trade in London at that time, I believe this was more a gesture of goodwill than a fact.

Sadly, the so-called mysteries of our Craft clearly and categorically do not exist in the form that we imagine and we as members are foolish to perpetuate that myth. In fact, in England during the middle-ages, it became the practice to call the trade skill of any artisan, a mystery, this word being taken from the Latin word *ministerium* meaning professional skill. So it is quite feasible to find a correlation between the words mystery and secret, and those words are still used together by today's Companies in the City of

London. Therefore it is sheer folly to accept this as being reference to the ancient mysteries of past civilisations as it purely relates to the trade skills. Sadly, as an organisation, we do ourselves a great injustice by weaving unnecessary webs of misconception that are unable to fully qualify or substantiate or that Grand Lodge do not recognise. An example of this is that over the last few years there have been two such theories that I overheard certain brethren speaking about. Both ideas disturbed me greatly and I believe insulted our Craft. They were the suggestions that 1) Jesus was a Freemason and 2) that the early Egyptians used Masonic symbols.

1) Since time immemorial there have been fraternities and associations of like-minded men, but there is simply no evidence to suggest that Freemasonry existed in those days of Christ. History does tell us however, that the simple yet moral life Jesus lived could be interpreted as the true aim of every Freemason, but that is the closest association we can even hope for.

2) As for the second theory which relates to the discovery of Masonic symbols found beneath the base of Cleopatra's needles situated in New York's Central Park and London's Embankment. This is exactly how Anderson wanted his organisation to be perceived, but there is no tangible evidence available to even remotely suggest they were Masonic symbols in the first place.

Having said that, whatever the exact history of Operative Masons might have been I cannot say and I believe it has been overlooked or lost probably because of the development of Andersons Free and Accepted Masonry. One example I can give of practices that Anderson overlooked or never understood relates to the Holy Royal Arch and the square and compass. Neville Barker Cryer tells us that from their earliest period, Operative Masons were always divided into two groups, Straight or Square Masons and Round or Arch Masons.

The reason for this was that the straight work needed less skill and therefore commanded less wages than that of the Round or Arch man whose ability to make arches, bridges an all kind of curved work commanded more skill and therefore more wages. There were seven grades within each:

Apprentice
Fellow of the Craft
Super Fellow
Super Fellow Erector

Super-Intendent
Passed Master
Master or Grand Master

Incidentally, the word degree does not appear in any of our records until about 1730, and then only in one of the early exposures. However, it has been a term constantly used since. The Apprentice to the Square Mason was logically given a square, obviously to check the accuracy of his work, while the Arch mason was given the compasses to assist him with making curves. The colour of the Square Mason was blue, whilst the Arch Mason was red and a lot of time and trouble could have been saved if this traditional fact was better known. These colours are clearly illustrated on the original coat of arms of the Society of the Free Masons granted by Edward VI. The one on the right side being a Square Mason, not only as you would expect, holding a square in his hand but also with blue-facings on his jacket. The one on the left was the Arch mason holding a pair of compasses along with red-facings on his jacket. Anderson either never knew about or never really understood this particular practice, which we now recognise as the beginnings of Royal Arch Masonry, and this was one of the contentions which lead to the formation of the Rival Grand Lodge in 1752, who practiced and developed the ritual of Royal Arch Masonry outside of the early Grand Lodge.

Surely we all realise that the use of Aprons, hoodwinks and cable tows for example, are widespread throughout primitive cultures, while customs such as the symbolic raising ceremony are not only commonly used, but representative of resurrection, reincarnation, re-birth and eternal life. In fact, that great badge of innocence and bond of friendship, the apron, which finds it origins and instigation in the Garden of Eden, has been common to all nations of the earth from the earliest periods of time. Thus, we find it formed part of the dress of the Isrealitish priesthood, Its ceremonial use was adopted by that of Mithras of Persia and the Indians of the Americas who presented aprons during their initiatory rites of its young braves

In India, the caste marks of Vishnu are characteristically that of the Junior Warden and are emphasised by the upright lines of the plumb-rule, likewise the caste marks of Shiva are parallel, like the level of the Senior Warden. Again in India and in parts of ancient Egypt, we find the Preserver in early mythology always depicted as trampling or stepping on the serpent of evil with his left foot.

Like Druidism, our Officers and perambulations can be said to imitate the worship of the sun. The Master, Senior and Junior Wardens all represent the position of the sun at crucial parts of the day, i.e. the rising, the meridian and the setting, while the candidate always follows its path; from east to west and our former religious Feast days also coincided with the Summer and Winter solstice. If we are to believe all legend, then the term "Mason" itself, is derived from the Druids in whose life the May-Pole played such an important role and who were known as "Men of May" or "Mays Sons".

And what about the words of Mencius, *c.*370 BC a contemporary of Confucius who wrote:

> *"A man should abstain from doing unto others what he would not wish they should do to him, this is called the principle of acting on the* square."

That little gem found its way into our Charge some 2,000 years later.

Many have falsely claimed that our ritual came through the Ancient mysteries of Isis and Osiris of Egypt, Mithras of Persia, Adonis of Syria, Dionysus, Bacchus, Eleusis and the dreams of the Grecian mythologists, but again, there is no evidence to prove these claims. Then we have that wonderful and most famous oration delivered by the Chevalier Andrew Michael Ramsey who in 1737 attributed Freemasonry to those knightly crusaders when he claimed the following, all without evidence of course:

- That Freemasonry arose in Palestine during the crusades and certain nobles made pledges to restore Christian Churches to the Holyland
- That when they returned to their own countries they would form Lodges with the same practical objective of the development of sacred architecture, i.e. the building of churches
- That there came a time when the Masonic order was neglected in most countries with the exception of England and especially Scotland
- That Scotland alone preserved the order and in 1286 the illustrious Mother Kilwinning arose from the mystical shadow of Mount Heredom

Needless to say once again man's mind went mad with these unfounded and romantic ideas, and in France particularly, we saw the formation a whole range of Chivalric and Christian Degrees. Many of these Degrees still exist and are practiced today in our Lodge rooms and although not officially recognised by Grand Lodge as being pure ancient Masonry, they are patronised by many eminent members of our Craft, and of course one must be a Freemason to join them.

This confusion concerning our origin has been most detrimental and damaging to our Craft particularly in later years when dangerous publications purporting to be Masonic in the nature, hit the book shops and become best sellers. For example, I site a recent publication entitled *Occult Powers* promoted in the following fashion:

> *"Divided into the three degrees of Apprentice, Journeyman or Fellowcraft and Master, the author presents a comprehensive textbook in developing your occult knowledge... The reader is lead to soul-searching through instructions that connect the yogic systems... the physiological and physic... in implementing higher exercises to learn the power of the Od... the apprentice exercise will give vital energy... the journeyman exercise helps us experience telepathy, higher breathing techniques, idealistic monism, dreams, clairvoyance clairaudience, and the healing power of magnetism... in the final development stage the reader is given the last key to see all things through the inner eye and thus become a master."*

Another publication entitled *The Secrets of Freemasonry,* is not much better for the author claims to have brought together Masonic tradition about the secrets connected with the Temple, and claims how mystical knowledge came into Freemasonry by the *"Charter of Larmanius"* which reveals a secret line of Knights Templar Grand Masters that have survived to the 19th century. He also asserts that there is a Secret Lodge which continues to teach *"true knowledge"* of the ancient mysteries and that the Craft transmits beliefs linked to the Earls of Rosslyn, the Knights Templars and Lodge Mother Kilwinning. At the bottom of the review we are told, the writer *"..has collected together this thread of belief from old Masonic writers and rewritten it in modern English to make the ideas accessible to modern readers."*

Sadly all this writer has done is to perpetuate myth and legend and regurgitate the same old material echoing my comments, that because Freemasonry has no historical origin, then one has to be found.

Now tonight brethren I have attempted to explain four points:

1) That some form of Speculative Masonry or Freemasonry was practiced in England between about 1620–1717

2) That Convivial Societies and Fraternities with the most wonderful sounding names were common place at the turn of the 18th century.

3) That James Anderson, father of Speculative Freemasonry as we know it, influenced and helped form the first Grand Lodge retrospectively, possibly as a Convivial Society first and in doing so, stole the existing history, practices and set-up of other groups to give his club credibility.

4) That subsequent to Andersons misuse of historical facts, Masonic scholars have wrongly invented the most fanciful and romantic theories of origin to give the Craft a credible history.

I would of course be very foolish to deny that there is evidence to suggest that some of our ritual and practices definitely and decidedly predate 1717, yet to what degree and in many cases, in what form, we are not sure. What we do know is that there is no evidence of a continued unbroken chain of Freemasonry handed down, as the ritual suggested since time immemorial. At the very least we can prove some association of non-trade persons, Freemen of the City/Borough, Gentry or Royalty with this fraternity since about 1595 in England, and 1600 in Scotland, but as time passes the chances of any further breakthrough in establishing many more facts that this are very slim.

For those brethren who continue to believe that Freemasonry has its origins in far flung places and since time immemorial I say this: You could be right, who knows where those rituals, practices, grips and signs originated. However, the Craft of Freemasonry, as practiced by us, in this room tonight, is no older than about 300 years and what we do in our Lodges may well be an imitation of the past practices...

> of warrior monks and Knights known as the knights
>> hospitallers
> of ancient pyramid builders
> of stone cutters from King Solomon's Temple
> of the Roman Colligia
> of the Comacine Masters of Italy
> of the Stienmetzens of Germany

of the French Compagnonnage
of the Monks of dissolved monasteries
of other Arcane or Esoteric schools
of the Company of Masons, the Company of Accepted Masons
or the Society of Free Masons

One thing we can be 100% sure about as I explained, there is no one group that has an unbroken record of passing on to successive groups those practices and whether we like it or not, our only starting reference point for our system of Speculative Freemasonry is 1717, and the formation of the first Grand Lodge, recoded retrospectively, by Dr James Anderson, from which all current Masonic practices emanate.

A lecture designed to answer many of the questions commonly asked about King Solomon's Temple

The Temple of King Solomon

(Written in 2009)

King Solomon's Temple! What was it? Where was it built? Why was it built? Who built it? Was it really Gods house? Who destroyed it? How long did it take to build? Why do some think it was never built in the first place?

Questions I have no doubt you have asked yourself since becoming acquainted with the building when you became a Freemason and which I have tried to cover in this lecture. To make the lecture easier to follow, I have broken it down into several easier to follow sections.

Israel

Israel, as you know, is a people and not a place, well not at least until about 1948 when after the holocaust and much to the chagrin of certain Middle Eastern states, world leaders felt it was both right and proper to restore a greatly scattered people to their so-called home land. Their original homeland, so the Bible suggests, was Mesopotamia until about 1750 BC when they were driven by famine into Egypt. Mesopotamia was approximately 300 miles long and 150 miles wide and is now modern-day Iraq. It was located between the Tigris and Euphrates rivers, which flow into the Persian Gulf. The word Mesopotamia means "the land between the rivers"

But it was while in Egypt, Israel was held in captivity and became slaves to that great ancient civilisation, the Egyptians, whose most fantastic building programme would no doubt have benefited from such a workforce. Their bondage lasted some 500 years until in 1250 BC when their great exodus, led by Moses, took them into the wilderness of Sinai where they escaped the clutches of Pharaoh and were directed by their great God, *Yahweh*, to the lush and fertile lands of Canaan. Canaan was a region which today encompasses modern-day Israel, Lebanon, the Palestinian territories and adjoining coastal lands, including parts of Jordan, Syria and north-eastern Egypt.

It was while in the mountains of Sinai, you will recall, that *Yahweh* spoke unto Moses and gave him the Ten Commandments and bade him to make a grand chest to keep them in. That grand chest, better known to us as the Ark of the Covenant, was made of wood and over laid with gold and was carried throughout their travels across the river Jordan and into the Promised Land. Wherever they camped, they placed the Ark in the tent called the Tabernacle which was a place for worship; the Ark represented the presence of God.

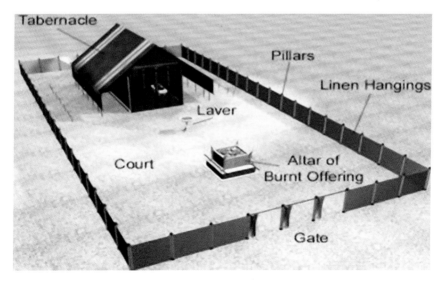

Records dating from the time of Ramses II make mention of a people called the *Apiru* (A-pir-ru) who were employed to build his new city and many have previously believed this refers to the Israelites, whom the Old Testament tells us were engaged in building works before their great exodus. Having said that, today's scholars explain the word *Apiru* (A-pir-ru) was a term used in both Syria and Mesopotamia to describe bandits, mercenaries, raiders and outcasts while in Egypt the term means "to bind" or "to make captive". Further Egyptian records from about 1209 BC state "Israel is laid waste, his seed is no more", and this is the only non-biblical reference to Israel at this time, and it details Pharaohs successful wars against the allied tribes of Israel.

In truth, there is nothing to confirm the accuracy of the great exodus, only what the Bible tells us, the story being recorded some 4–500 years after the events. The general view these days is that the Israelites where exactly that, a group or caste of renegade bandits and mercenaries who settled in Canaan and who slowly took over the whole area, which they called their "promised land".

Jerusalem

Long before Jerusalem was to become the centre of the Jewish world, it was no more than a remote mountain site, used from about 3200 BC as a burial area with little or no sign of inhabitants or town life. To the west was the land of Canaan and to the east the Jordan River and the ancient walled city of Jericho. As the area slowly became settled, it was found to have a natural protection, because of its position, and a fresh water supply from the Gihon (ghee-khone) spring which flowed from the east.

From the earliest of times, this area was sacred as all hills and mountains in the ancient Middle East were, this is because they reached high into the sky. The Ophel (off-ell) hill, upon which Jerusalem was built was no exception to this and was linked to the Syrian God, Shalem, a deity associated with the setting sun or the evening star.

But these were turbulent times for this area as there was a great climate change which caused the vast migration of Sea people that originated beyond the Black Sea, to start their movement east. As these migrations took place, so entire civilisations were overthrown including the Mycenaean's of Greece and the Hittites, but it was the Jebusites, who were probably the remnants of the Hittites, that chose to settle in the highlands

MAP OF THE PERIOD OF THE KINGS

Bible History Online

of Judah while the Philistines settled along the coastal lowlands of Canaan. At the same time as this, another group, back from their escape from Egypt, namely the Israelites, were also trying to settle and soon encircled the Jebusite settlement at Jerusalem.

By 1020 BC Saul immerged as the first King of the northern tribes, known as Israel, but upon his death, the Elders approached David, who was the King of the tribes situated in the south, known as Judah to become their King. The United Kingdom of Judah and Israel had now totally encircled the small area held by the Jebusites. The capital of the kingdom of Judah was Hebron, 20 miles south of Jerusalem. Hebron's importance was due to the belief that it was the burial place of Abraham and other great ancestors of the Israelites, but after just a few years as king of both Israel and Judah, David, conquered the Jebusite town of Jerusalem and from there, so the Bible tells us, ruled over all of the kingdom of Israel for the next 33 years.

David's decision to make Jerusalem the capital of his kingdom was more likely due to the fact that it was neutral, inasmuch that it neither belonged to Judah or Israel and none of the 12 tribes had any religious or political claims on the city. In fact, after the conquest, it became a mixed city for instead of expelling the Canaanites or the Hittites, they dwelt among them making it a city of mixed inhabitants, perfect for him to rule over his kingdom.

The Ark of the Covenant

We have already learnt that while in the mountains of Sinai, Yahweh spoke unto Moses, gave him the Ten Commandments and bade him to make a grand chest to keep them in. That grand chest, better known to as the Ark of the Covenant, was made of wood and over laid with gold. We also learnt that it was carried throughout their travels and where ever they camped, they placed the Ark in the tent called the Tabernacle. The Ark represented the presence of God.

Now that he was settled in Jerusalem, David wanted it to become the centre of the people's religious life so he ordered the Ark to be brought into the city to be given a permanent home in a building, i.e. a temple or house of God. But David's plans met with opposition from the prophet Nathan who announced that God never needed a temple when the tribes were wandering in the desert and he did not need one now and with regard to the building of a house to God, God in fact would establish a house of David, a dynasty from which the Messiah would come. But Gods refusal was only temporary; it was because David was not a suitable person to build a temple because he was a warrior king with blood on his hands, he was only allowed to choose the site for the building, the honour of building the temple would belong to his son, Solomon.

The Threshing Floor of Zion

Just north of David's city, which as we know was built on the Ophel hill, was a higher and taller summit known as Zion which belonged to a Jebusite named *Araunah*. During a plague which killed 70,000 people in three days, an angel appeared to David and stood on the threshing floor of *Araunah,* which was at the summit of the mount. David quickly recognised the fact that as well as using the threshing floors to separate the chaff from the wheat, the Jebusites used their threshing floors for prophetic divination, worship and appeasement of their storm god Baal. David therefore decided he must build an altar there and by paying for the land, the altar, and the oxen to be sacrificed, he would in fact ensure that the sacrifice would be without obligation to anyone but Yahweh, his god. From that point on, the site of the Temple was clearly marked out, but scholars continue to debate the exact position.

But whatever the arguments, this piece of land where the Jebusites made sacrifices to the god Baal, now became the place where the holy of holies would be built, that innermost sanctum of the Temple on that great rock, which can still be seen today in the Dome of the Rock on Temple Mount.

Muslims say it was this same spot where Mohammed ascended on his Night Journey to Paradise. Orthodox Jews claim it was where Abraham was commanded to sacrifice his son Isaac. It was also the place also where David ultimately brought the Ark of the Covenant.

King Solomon's Temple

Over the next few years, David consolidated his position. Having already combined the kingdoms of Judah and Israel, roughly where Israel stands today, he also subdued the kingdoms of Edom and Moab in the east and Damascus in the north. Today the areas of western Jordan, southern Lebanon, and central Syria were all once part of David's empire but are now countries in their own right.

King Solomon, David's son, extended the city of Jerusalem to include the holy mount and began a large and ambitious building programme which included a palace complex for his huge harem of 700 princesses, the 300 concubines, who were gifts from foreign rulers and a grand palace for his Egyptian wife. He built a large armoury, a judgement hall and on the ancient threshing floor which once belonged to the old Jebusite, *Araunah*, he built the Temple.

Building a temple was no mean feat and the Bible tells us that Solomon ordered 30,000 Israelites to be divided into three groups of 10,000 and working in shifts they cut timber in Lebanon for a month, and then worked for two months in Jerusalem, while another 80,000 were sent into the mountains to quarry stone for the foundations as a further 70,000 porters carried the stone to the site. There were 3,300 supervisors overseeing the building work. The construction which began in the fourth year of Solomon's reign, took seven years and five months to complete which would have been from about the spring of 958 BC to the autumn of 951 BC. We can also read in the Bible how the Temple was rectangle in shape, oriented on an east west axis and measured 60 cubits in length, 20 cubits in width and 30 cubits in height.

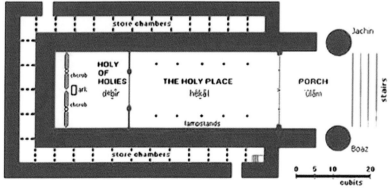

A cubit was the length of a man's arm from his elbow to the tip of his middle finger, about half a yard. Therefore, we can roughly say that the Temple was approximately 30 yards long, 10 yards wide and 15 yards high, which does not seem to be such a large building. The purpose of temples in the ancient world was to provide a dwelling place for god, and as with all temples in the East during that period, their design was based on an ordinary house. King Solomon's Temple was built with three chambers and progressing inwards each chamber was more holy and more sacred than the previous.

The first or outer most chamber was known as the *ulam* which we know as the porch way or entrance. This led to the *hekal* or middle chamber where according to Masonic legend the fellow Crafts went to receive their wages. Also kept here were various items including a gold altar, ten candelabra, various lamps, goblets, cups, knives, basins and braziers. The middle chamber led directly to the *debir*, a windowless chamber 20 cubits long, wide, and high, a perfect cube. This was the Holy of Holies, closed by folding doors where Yahweh claimed he would dwell. Here was the Ark of the Covenant with two huge cherubim or angels with wings either side. This spot was so sacred that any contact with the Ark without several washings and anointing and taking the proper precautions would result in immediate death. The building itself was not what one would consider remarkable, being about a quarter of the size of the Parthenon in Athens, which was built about 500 years later, but what was so special about Solomon's Temple was the costly fine worked materials and decoration, which Solomon relied upon his friend and ally, Hiram King of Tyre, to supply.

Hiram King of Tyre

Tyre, was an ancient and successful Mediterranean seaport on the coast of Lebanon which had long been trading with Egypt, Sicily, North and East Africa and Arabia. Hiram and Solomon were great friends; Hiram had been friends with David and had already helped him with the construction of his own palace, they traded with each other and together as partners. Hiram consolidated that friendship by allowing the marriage of one of his daughters to Solomon. Although David had been forbidden to build the temple, he had amassed a great amount of treasure to pay for its construction, as well as materials and had made detailed plans. Knowing his father had received help from Hiram when building his own palace, Solomon turned to the old family friend for help.

The forests of Lebanon were rich in pine, juniper and cedar, all tall trees valuable in construction. The Pyramids of Giza were built with the aid of cedar beams from Lebanon, as were the great solar boats buried in the tomb of Cheops, and now Hiram provided Solomon with cedar for his Temple. But not only did Hiram provide the timber, he also provided craftsmen who panelled the interior of the Temple, lined the Holy of Holies with pure gold and then overlaid the entire exterior with more gold. One such craftsman was set to become more remarkable than any other, he was also called Hiram.

Hiram the Widows Son

Of all the work carried out in the Temple, nothing was more remarkable than the enormous basin known as the Sea of Bronze and the two huge bronze pillars named Jachin and Boaz. In those days, casting on such a large scale was both difficult and technically advanced and the man sent by King Hiram to carry out the work was described as being "filled with wisdom and understanding" and "a widow's son", better known to us in the Masonic setting as Hiram Abiff.

The Sea of Bronze was used for ritual washings and stood on the back of 12 oxen representing the twelve tribes of Israel. It was about five yards in diameter and almost three yards high and held about 10,000 gallons of water. The two hollow bronze pillars stood some nine yards high, were free standing and placed either side of the porch way or entrance which led to the middle chamber. As you will recall they were each surmounted with capitals some two and half yard's high, making the pillars approximately 11 and a half yards high. The capitals as you recall were adorned with lily work and pomegranates and were used as incense burners and torch holders. They were cast in the valley of Jordan where there was earth to make the moulds, water in abundance and wind to fans the flames of the furnaces.

Hiram, the widow's son gave the pillars names, the pillar on the South side, which if we stand facing the Worshipful Master becomes our right side, he called Jachin, meaning "He shall establish" and the Pillar on the North side which if we stand facing the Worshipful Master becomes our left side, he called Boaz, meaning "In it is strength". In the Masonic setting, we understand this to mean "In strength I will establish this mine house to stand firm forever." Actually, there is no record in any scripture of God saying these words, and historians and students alike have interpreted these words as referring to the House of David from which the Messiah came.

At the end of the building of the Temple, the fate of Hiram, the widow's son is unknown as the Bible allows him to leave quietly and nothing more is said about him. However, in the Masonic setting he is slain after demonstrating fidelity, one of the greatest principles of Freemasonry.

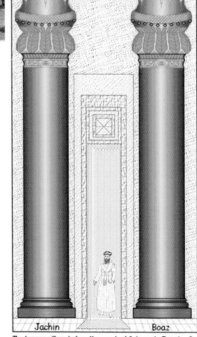

The bronze pillars before the porch of Solomon's Temple. On the right was Jachin; on the left Boaz – *I Kings 7:21*

A House for the Name of God

When the building was finally completed, it was dedicated by Solomon who tells us that he "built the house for the name of the Lord God". The Temple was not a dwelling place for God, as the Israelitish God was without form and was everywhere, neither could he be contained, nor did he have a representative image, for the Temple contained no images. This was actually unheard of in the ancient world as all shrines or temples had images to be worshipped. The only thing contained in the Temple at Jerusalem was the name of God, and legend tells us that this could never be uttered only at certain times by priests that had undergone many ceremonies of purification. The Ark of the Covenant which was kept in the Holy of Holies merely symbolised the presence of God.

The destruction of the First Temple and the building and destruction of the Second Temple

What little information I could find about the destruction of the first Temple indicates that it was sacked by the Assyrians in 586 BC. However, legend has it that the Ark of the Covenant had long since disappeared.

When the Persians overran Babylonia in 536 BC, the Persian ruler Cyrus the Great issued a proclamation allowing the Jews to return to Judea and rebuild the Temple. Zerubbable was the leader of the first group of 50,000 Jews who according to God's promise came back from exile to rebuild God's temple. Despite extremely difficult conditions, the Jews completed rebuilding the Temple in 515 BC and the Jews lived relatively peacefully in Jerusalem, with their holy Temple serving as a religious center. However, the second Temple was never to regain the presence of God in the form of the Ark, it was a vast empty place which instead, became the house of a completely spiritualised deity.

The Second Temple suffered desecration by Antiochus Epiphanes in 167 BC but was rededicated under Judas Maccabaeus in 164 BC. Centuries later in around 20 BC, the building was renovated by Herod the Great, and became known as Herod's Temple. During the Roman occupation of Judah, the Temple remained under control of the Jewish High Priest. It was later destroyed by the Romans in 70 AD during the Siege of Jerusalem.

The Obliteration

By AD 135, all traces of the once glorious Temple were gone. Statues of Hadrian and Jupiter were erected on the site which marked the final insult.

Jews were forbidden by Roman decree to enter Jerusalem and only as an unspoken gesture could they visit the rubble which was all that remained and the desolate rock, where the Jews poured their religious oils, offered prayers and tore their clothes in lamentation.

Answering those Questions

So to conclude this lecture, let me answer the questions we posed at the start.

What was it? Solomon tells us that he "built the house for the name of the Lord God". It was not a dwelling place for God, but it did contain His name, and you recall that legend tells us that this could never be uttered only at certain times by priests that had undergone many ceremonies of purification.

Where was it built? Just north of Jerusalem was a higher summit known as Zion which belonged to a Jebusite named *Araunah*. During the plague which killed 70,000 people, an angel appeared to David and stood on the threshing floor of *Araunah* which was at the summit of the mount. David quickly recognised that the Jebusites used their threshing floors for prophetic divination. David built an altar there and sacrificed oxen and from that point the area was clearly marked as the spot for the Temple site.

Why was it built? Quite simply to house the Ark of the Covenant which was kept in the Holy of Holies, which contained the name of God and symbolised the presence of God,

Who built it? It was instigated by David, but as he was considered a warrior king with blood on his hands, the responsibility fell upon his son Solomon.

Was it really Gods house? As we know, the Temple was not a dwelling place for God, as the Israelitish God was without form, neither did he have a representative image, which was actually unheard of in the ancient world as all shrines or temples had images to be worshipped. As we have learnt it contained only name of God, Yahweh, probably better known to us as *Jehovah* and the Ark of the Covenant which symbolised the presence of God. So, whether you think it to be the house of God is for you to decide.

How long did it take to build? The construction began in the fourth year of Solomon's reign, took seven years and five months to complete, which as we have heard was from the spring of 958 BC to the autumn of 951 BC

Who destroyed it? The first Temple sacked by the Assyrians in 586 BC. Legend has it that the Ark of the Covenant had long since disappeared. The Second Temple built by Zerubbable and completed in 515 BC, was desecrated in 167 BC. Although rededicated 164 BC. and renovated by Herod the Great around 20 BC, when it the became known as "Herod's Temple." It was finally destroyed by the Romans in 70 AD during the Siege of Jerusalem and by 135 AD, all traces of the once glorious Temple were gone.

Why do some think it was never built in the first place? Students of the Temple of Jerusalem seem to fall into two camps, half take the building of the Temple literally and using the biblical story, believe this once sacred building, of which all that remains is found under the Dome of the Rock, to be a factual account of events. Others believe the house that God intended to build was the House of David, a symbolical house from which would descend the Messiah. So again, it is for the student himself to decide.

Finally, brethren, in the Masonic setting, our representation of the building of King Solomon's Temple is purely allegorical and bears little or no resemblance to the biblical story. Likewise, there is nothing whatsoever to suggest that there is any connection between our ritual and the ceremonies practiced in the temple of old and we are wrong to make that assumption. Our association with the Temple or rather its chief architect is purely a lesson in unshakable fidelity, where Hiran Abiff chooses to sacrifice his own life rather than to pass on the secrets of the Degree.

A dramatic, but primitive and almost primeval reconstruction of absolute loyalty to an association which never really contained any secrets in the first place, and that brethren as we know, has always been our most closely guarded secret of all.

Why the Knights Templar were not the Founders or the Custodians of the Secrets of Freemasonry.

(Written in 2011)
Based on the writings of Robert L. D. Cooper, author of
The Rosslyn Hoax.

Those of you that remember my 2009 Cornwallis lecture "Surviving History", will recall how I established the fact that Freemasonry had suffered at the hands of many an eminent Masonic historian whose sole aim was to create a history for Speculative Freemasonry where there had not been one previously, and in doing so influenced Masonic writers well into the early 21st century. I also highlighted one of the more enduring historical theories which were the belief that the Craft originated in the encampments of the Knights Templar and that they alone were the founders of Freemasonry.

I also established through my research, that although many brethren believe there is a Templar link, very few have actually read any books on the subject, preferring to "take the word" of somebody else or just accept the theory because it seemed plausible and of course, it flattered the organisation to which they belong.

This is, I believe, an indictment on our society, and the paradox of having many brethren crafted in the delivery of rote learnt ritual, yet lacking any understanding of what they are actually doing or where those traditions originated. But the education of our brethren is not a subject to discuss lightly, nor is it the subject of this lecture.

Our question in this lecture being: Where did the idea come from that the Knights Templar were the founders or the custodians of our secrets and what is the connection between the Freemasons and the Knights Templar? Firstly, let's briefly examine the historical background of the Knights Templar.

- In 1095, Pope Urban II called the first crusade at Clermont in France.
- By 1099, the Crusaders had captured Jerusalem.
- In 1118, Hugh de Payens and Godfrey de Saint-Omer, form a community with seven other knights to protect pilgrims. Baldwyn II, King of Jerusalem, provide them with quarters thought to be in the grounds or even near the remains of King Solomon's Temple.
- First known as the Poor Knights of Christ, they later became the Knights of the Temple.
- The next 200 years see the Order receive full Papal blessing, grow in membership and riches, but ultimately lose their place in Jerusalem to Saladin.
- The Order became extremely rich and powerful throughout central Europe, out growing their original ethos as the Poor Knights of Christ and allegedly becoming corrupt.
- By 1307, Philip VI of France, now heavily in debt saw an opportunity to seize their wealth and on Friday 13 October 1307, ordered their arrest and handed them over to the Inquisition.

- By 1308, a Papal Bull was issued calling for the arrest of all Knights Templar.
- In 1312, in Scotland, Robert the Bruce was under excommunication from the Church and therefore the Papal Bull was ignored by the King. It is believed that this led to the Templar's from France to take refuge in Scotland some, in particular, with the St Clair's of Rosslyn.
- In 1314, legend has it that the Templar support received by the King led to the famous Scottish victory over the English at Bannockburn.
- Legend also has it that they settled in Portugal, some even in America, but more crucially at this point they enter the realms of myth and legend and we find no further records of them.

Having given a very brief outlook of this Order let us now look briefly at the development of Freemasonry, in particular our association with the Temple at Jerusalem, from which the Knights Templar took their name.

- We know for a fact that prior to 1717, many of the *Old Manuscript Constitutions* which contained the legendary history of the Freestone or Operative Masons contained little or no mention what so ever about the building of King Solomon's Temple.
- We know that there are contained in some, of the *Old Manuscript Constitutions* brief details of the building of the Tower of Babel and the City of Nineveh, but nothing in any great detail.
- We know that the *Old Manuscript Constitutions* are all of English origin.
- We know that other pre-1717 Masonic documents from Scotland, contain details of do how to make a Mason, giving the Mason word and the five points of fellowship, but do not contain the legendary history nor details of the of the building of King Solomon's Temple.

So, we can earnestly say that the building of King Solomon Temple was not the main thrust of late 17th and early 18th century Freemasonry. So when did this introduction take place?

Nobody can really say, but the first introduction we have of the Hiram story starts in about 1730. So logically, if the old ritual documents from Scotland dated 1696–1710 make no mention of King Solomon's Temple and the first record we have of the legend on English Soil about 1730, what does that tell us?

- That the story was older than 1710, but younger than 1730.
- That at the revival of Freemasonry in about 1717, the ritual appears only to contain the Apprentice and Fellow grades or an Acception ceremony, but no mention of the Hiramic legend.
- That these ceremonies were carried over from the practices of the 17th century Company, Society or Fellowship of Freemasons, Accepted Mason or just Masons, all these titles are mentioned between 1620 and 1688.
- That term "degree" was not a Masonic term, until it was introduced in a Masonic Exposure in 1730, neither did the ritual contain the Hiram legend or its association with King Solomon's Temple until that date.
- That the Hiramic legend or our association with King Solomon was probably an English innovation developed between 1724, when we have the first record of a third grade taking place, and 1730, when we find the story in print. (It is worth noting that we do not have the content of the ritual delivered in the 1724 ceremony and strangely enough it was actually carried out in an unrecognised quasi-Masonic organisation called The Society for the appreciation of Music and Architecture)
- We must also take note that in the *"Graham Manuscript"*, dated 24 October 1726, there is reference to the loss and apparent search for the lost secrets known only to Noah, very similar and in the same vain as the traditional history of the current Third Degree, illustrating at least that the Hiramic Legend had possibly yet to be fully constructed.

Now, as much of the practices and superstitions of the new 1717 Grand Lodge organisation contained remnants which were inherited from the pre-1717 *Old Manuscript Constitutions* we find that so was the pre-reformation religious influence.

This, as we know, did not suit early Masonic activists like Dr James Anderson nor John Desagulier, both of whom were Protestant Ministers, and whom set out to remove the Catholic or pre-reformation religious influence from the early organisation. This has been called by some as "The De-Christianising of the Craft". This continued well up to the time of the Grand Master ship of the Duke of Sussex, almost a century later, who it appeared, had not wanted to offend several of his influential Jewish friends.

By 1730, Freemasonry had begun to spread throughout Europe and Grand Lodges were set up in France, Germany and the Netherlands to name but a few countries. However, for the purpose of this lecture, I wish to concentrate on France, who unlike its neighbours England and Germany, was a strong Catholic Country. For many Catholic brethren in France, the de-Christianising of Freemasonry left a great void and it was at this point that France became a fertile ground or the epicentre of what was to become a whole range of religious Degrees and chivalrous Orders.

So, to briefly recap at this stage, let us see what the facts we have established thus far. We know that:

- The Templar's formed in 1118 and later, charged with heresy and disbanded in 1307, those that were not killed fled, some it is believed went to Scotland.
- In 1717, Freemasonry had, what some consider, a revival in London and at first adopted some of the practices found in the *"Old Manuscript Constitutions"* which contained the legendary history of the Freestone or Operative masons.
- At a later point other pre-1717 documents from Scotland become available that did not contain the legendary history, but did contain details of how to make a Mason, giving the Mason word and the five points of fellowship. These confirmed early English Masonic practices.
- That the removing of the pre-reformation influence and de-Christianising of the Craft caused France to become the epicentre of a whole range of religious Degrees and chivalrous orders.

It was what happened next that caused people to consider that Freemasonry had more romantic origins than just an association with the pre-reformation builder's trade. In France Freemasons at the time were generally from the middle and upper classes or the higher echelons of society, therefore a knightly connection proved too hard to resist, and as Anderson himself had already given the Craft a false belief of great antiquity so such a suggestion was readily acceptable.

This suggestion came in 1737, when Scotsman, Andrew Ramsey, a Jacobite exile, living in France, introduced the fictitious notion that Freemasonry had a crusader background. However, the Freemasonry as founded in Britain, as you are all well acquainted with, was made up of artisans and aristocrats alike, its members contained professional and learned men, including middle-class tradesmen, all of whom were happy to rub shoulders together.

It France however, it seems conversely, that the upper-strata of French society were not content with belonging to a society or fraternity that had grown from such humble workingman's beginnings, they wanted something better, they wanted recognition and social distinction and they wanted it with style, nostalgia and sheer romance. This came when Ramsey claimed in his Oration to St John's Lodge in Paris that:

> *"Our ancestors, the crusaders, who had come from all parts*
> *of Christendom to the Holy Land, wanted to group persons*
> *from every nation in a spiritual confraternity."*

And in one fail swoop, he turned French Freemasonry into an ancient and international chivalrous secret society.

Ramsey went on to claim that the Crusaders had attempted to restore or rebuild the Temple in such a hostile environment that they devised a set of secret signs that would stop their Muslim enemies from infiltrating them. After their defeat by Saladin, the Crusaders returned home and established Freemasons Lodges. However, the Lodges in England fell into neglect and it was only among the Scots that Freemasonry preserved its former splendour. He claimed that although Great Britain had been the seat of the Order:

> *"The Royal Art had now passed to France and France alone*
> *would cloth the Order, with grace, delicacy and good taste*
> *and that all nations and strangers will learn that France is*
> *the home of all nations."*

Up until this point, he only ever claimed that there was a crusader link with Freemasonry, however in papers found after his death and published in

Glasgow in 1749 he claimed, "…every Mason is a Knight Templar…" a remark that was never forgotten.

So, in 1760, when a Frenchman who pretended to be George Frederick Johnson, a Scottish Nobleman, told German Freemasons that he had access to Templar Secrets, he was welcomed with open arms as Germany too was an old fashion society dominated by notions of rank. Johnson claimed that the Templar Grand Masters spent their time in the East learning the secrets and acquiring treasure, mainly from the Jewish Essences. These secrets and treasures were handed down from Grand Master to Grand Master and so to Jacques de Molay, who just happens, according to the story, to be known as Hiram.

Johnson claimed that on the night before his execution, Molay ordered a group of Templars', who were still at large, to enter the crypt of the Paris Temple and make off with the treasure. This treasure was said to contain the seven-branched candelabra used in the Jerusalem Temple as well as the Crown of the King of Jerusalem and a shroud. These treasures were taken to La Rochelle where 18 Templar galleys lay in wait to take them to the Isle of Mull where the Templar's started to called themselves, Freemasons.

With regard to Jacques de Molay, he was burnt to death on the evening of 18 March 1314 and legend has it that as the flames engulfed him he called for vengeance and demanded the King of France and the Pope, both co-conspirators in the fall of the Templar's, to appear with him before the throne of God in one year and a day. There is, as you would expect, no contemporary evidence of these threats being made, however, the one eye witness account that we do have, written by a monk, explains that he went to his death, "…with easy mind and will…".

Nevertheless, five weeks later on 20 April, Pope Clement V died of the long and painful illness that had affected him throughout his pontificate and on 29 November King Phillip IV died after falling from his horse while hunting.

Now it does not take too much imagination to guess what came next. Yes! You are right! Conspiracy theorists of all ages have claimed that the Jacques de Molay's curse brought about the deaths of both the King and the Pope, not forgetting the French revolution of 1789 which brought down the French Royal family while humbling the great Catholic Church, and all attributed to de Molay, and the remnants of a few renegade Templar's working through Freemasonry.

This was the belief of Charles de Gassicour, who claimed in a book published in 1796, that at the guillotining of Louis XVI, somebody shouted, "Jacques de Molay, you are avenged". It was de Gassicour who claimed that de Molay had founded four Lodges in Edinburgh and that the Templers and Freemasons were associated with the infamous Assassins, that they supported the protestant Oliver Cromwell and that it was they alone that stormed the Bastille.

Further fuel was added to the fire in 1797, when Abbe Augustin Barruel wrote the following:

> *"...a certain number of guilty knights, having escaped, ... united for the preservation of their horrid mysteries...to which they added the vow against the kings and priests who destroyed their order...These mysteries have descended to you, (the Freemasons) and you continue to perpetuate their impiety, their vows and their oaths. Such is your origin."*

Perhaps realising himself that there was a distinct lack of corresponding evidence in making this link between Templar's and Freemasons, he adds:

> *"The lapse of time and the change of manners have varied a part of your symbols and your frightful systems, but the essence of them remains, the vows, the oaths, the hatred and the conspiracies are the same."*

A few years later, Barruel adds the Jews to his theory, seeing them as the real power behind the Freemasons and the ultimate manipulation of European events, a theory which festered in Europe, particularly in Germany until the rise of the Third Reich.

Barruel himself was an exile from revolutionary France, living in London where he was clever enough to thank the British Government for granting him asylum and was generous enough to claim that these activities in France did not apply to the respectable Freemasons of Britain.

As I previously explained in the first section, France became the epicentre of new Orders and Degrees and just prior to that, London itself, was awash with other fraternities, clubs or convivial societies many of which had their own joining criteria and signs as we learn from an article found in the *Tatler*, dated 1709 which talks about a group having; "...signes and tokens like Freemasons".

However, in France, there sprung up about 30 or so Orders and Degrees all purporting to be Masonic, some full of mysticism, some religious and others chivalric and among them was the Knights Templar degree.

At first, both the English and Scottish Grand Lodges dismissed the degree as being a foreign corruption of the more tradition Freemasonry being practised.

But in 1843, the Order of the Knights Templar in Scotland published a treatise in which they gave an account of their origins and how the Templar's joined the standard of Robert the Bruce at Bannockburn in 1314, to help him secure the throne. According to the account, just three months after the burning of de Molay, the Templar's charged against the English at a decisive moment which gave victory to the Scots. The king naturally wishing to help preserve the Order protected them by transforming them into a new Order, the Freemasons. Of course, as usual, none of this alleged history had been recorded by any contemporary Scottish chronicler and the whole story appears to have been made up in the 19th century. In fact, as you will all see, the Scottish Freemasons had done no more than what English Freemasons had been doing since the previous century and that was to give themselves a credible history and a rather flattering one at that.

We all understand that every branch of Freemasonry and its Appendant Orders has its own story or traditional history which underpins that particular Masonic system. None of these traditional histories were intended to be taken seriously, but are allegorical and designed to illustrate the salient points of the Order. However, sadly as we know, these histories are passed down and told with such passion that each Freemason accepts them without question, and that is when it becomes dangerous. An example of this was in 1859, in his book *History of Free Masonry* Alexander Laurie passes over the Templar-Freemasonry link by saying:

> *"To prove that the Order of the Knights Templar was a branch of Freemasonry would be a useless labour, as the fact has been invariably acknowledged by Freemasons themselves."*

This as you now know, was not the case, and this did no more than fuel the myth of the Knights Templar connection which lingered on and began to take its more modern shape.

A central event in the Scottish Templar history had to be established, Bannockburn now became that central event. Now what was needed was a place, and that evolved in 1982 with the publication of *The Holy Blood and The Holy Grail* followed by *The Hiram Key, The Templar Revelation* and so on, which now began to identify Rosslyn Chapel, as the repository of the most powerful and iconic Templar treasures: The embalmed head of Jesus Christ, the Ark of the Covenant and the Holy Grail, and so on.

The legend now even starts to suggest that the Templar's discovered America. Evidence found in Rosslyn Chapel in the shape of carvings of "maize" and the "aloe cactus", both plants of the New World, seem to seem to suggest that Rosslyn which was built in 1456 almost 50 years before Columbus discovered America, was influenced by those that must have been familiar with or had visited the New World.

The story is further compounded by the old stone tower at Newport, Rhode Island. The Newport Tower which stands on arches and is believed by some to be a Templar Church built by Templar Colonists that came to America.

Some theorists believe that the Templar's landed there after the suppression of their order in about 1308 and their subsequent fleeing from La Rochelle. Other have also suggested that it was Henry Sinclair, a Templar, and his son William Sinclair, Lord of Roslyn that took charge of a voyage by the Venetian brothers, Nicolo and Antonio Zeno who in maps and letters, claim to have reached Nova Scotia in 1389.

Such are some of the theories proposed in 1996, in the book *The Hiram Key* by Christopher Knight and Robert Lomas. But to some, there are problems with such theories. The carvings, for example, do not necessarily look like "maize" and we accept the author's argument or interpretation as fact. Likewise, botanists will claim that the "aloe cactus" is actually a succulent and not a cactus and that it is a native of Africa, not America, and the other crucial factor is that it could not survive the harsh winters in the areas of New England that were supposedly discovered or settled the Templar's.

As for the carvings, architects and building surveyors will be quick to point out that these, and other carvings, were not carved into the stone fabric of the building, but were carved on stone plaques of some type and at a later point and attached or fixed in place, making the dating process unreliable.

In 1677, the owner of the so-called Newport Tower, records the building as being "my stone built windmill" and two excavations on the site in 1951 and 2006 concluded that the tower was built between 1650 and 1670. The Zeno brother's alleged voyage was, according to letters and maps, in 1558, but the documents associated with this voyage are now considered by many to be a hoax. The suggestion that Henry Sinclair and friends also made that trip is also spurious, as we are told in the 2002, *New Orkney Antiquarian Journal* that:

> *"Henry Sinclair, an earl of Orkney of the late fourteenth century, did not go to America. It was not until 500 years after Henry's death that anybody suggested that he did. The sixteenth century text that gave rise to the claims about Henry and America certainly did not say so. What it says in so many words is that someone called Zichmni, with friends, made a trip to Greenland. None of Henry Sinclair's contemporaries or near contemporaries ever claimed that he went to America; and none of the antiquaries who wrote about him in the seventeenth century said so either, although they made other absurd claims about him. The story is a modern myth, based on careless reading, wishful thinking and sometimes distortion, and during the past five years or so it has taken on new outrageous forms."*

Another theory claims that the Templar voyage to America was undertaken in ships of their fleet, part of that same fleet that sailed for Scotland from Northern France. There is no doubt that the Templar's had ships, particularly to carry pilgrims, personnel and supplies from Marseilles to Acre, but these were not ocean-going vessels, neither were they designed to carry water for more than a day of two. Likewise, they may well have had three of four galleys or warships, but whatever the case, the so-called Templar fleet would have been based at Marseilles in the Mediterranean as that was without a doubt their main sea port.

Historians also now cast doubt that there would have been any of the Templar fleet at La Rochelle in the first place, dispelling that other myth and or course that other piece of invented history that when the fleet made its escape, they hoisted their red "Skull and Crossbones" and continued to resist the Papacy and Crowned heads of Europe by living the lives of pirates on the high seas.

As ever, a closer examination of the theories of those eminent historians and writers quickly leave so much room for doubt.

In conclusion, since my very first lecture entitled "Stealing History" written and presented in 2001 to my 2009 Cornwallis Lecture, entitled "Surviving History" I have often felt that I have been a lone voice defending the fact that Freemasonry is not a supernatural society, hiding the true secrets of life or the whereabouts of the grail. It is not based on any mysticism or the occult. It has no religious or political agenda nor does it attempt to introduce a New World Order. It has no secrets.

It is, a mutual improvement society based on the standard beliefs of all religions which are: Love the Lord your God, whosoever you perceive him to be and serve your fellow man, and if you have joined Freemasonry on any other premise, then you have joined the wrong organisation.

Obviously, a by-product of this ethos is friendship, companionship, loyalty and hard work and we must never underestimate the personal joy we all receive from service to others, but attempting to attach some sort of romantic hypothesis to our origins is wrong, and making money from the publication of those outrageous theories is also likewise wrong. Likewise, it does nothing to enhance the ethos of our fraternity, often actually detracting from it.

Most authors will consider any subject to publish "fair game" and sadly, Freemasonry has been no exception to this and if you couple this with the fact that to most brethren, their introduction to religious history and the building of King Solomon's Temple comes through the ritual alone, then we will always be on a hiding to nothing.

The ritual as we are all told, was never meant to be a factual account of true events, but a tradition and colourful story of the degree being worked and we must never forget one of the questions we are asked as we prove our competence to move to the degree of a Fellowcraft:

Q) What is Freemasonry?
A) A peculiar system of morality veiled in allegory and illustrated by symbols.

That does not change as we progress in Freemasonry or join other Orders, they are still "veiled in allegory", and therefore must be accepted as such.

The moral of this lecture is simple, do not to get involved in invented historical theories until you know the truth, and that, you only achieve through personal study, ever recalling that day when we all joined this wonderful fraternity and were told:

"...to study more especially such of the liberal Arts and Sciences as may lie within the compass of our attainment, and without neglecting the ordinary duties of our station, to endeavour to make a daily advancement in Masonic knowledge."

That charge brethren, is not rescinded no matter what high office we attain or what other Degree's we join.

English Accepted Masonry
versus
Scottish Non-Operative Masonry
(Written in 2013)

It was a year or two ago, in response to a Lecture we had received in my Mark Lodge, that I struck up a debate with a Right Worshipful Brother of Scottish decent. It concerned which country first began the practice of admitting men by Acception or as a Non-Operative member into what can best be described as a Masons Lodge or Lodge of Operative Masons. Of course, the Right Worshipful Brother being proud of his own Scottish heritage, was keen to cite Scotland. Me? Well I have an Irish heritage, but I put that aside to cite England as my choice.

At this stage I have eliminated all other countries as there are no other records of fraternities or societies growing out of any old artisan organisations. Although the French Companionage, the German Stienmetzen, the Italian Commacine Masters and the Roman Collegia, possibly being the exception, but having little or no resemblance to those organisations which lately developed from the said trade organisation in the British Isles. In fact, as news reached the continent of the formation of Grand Lodge, so Freemasonry was initially imported from Britain and worked in those countries, under our Grand Lodge, until they quickly established their own Grand Lodges, which in most cases was from about 1730 onwards. But we must step further back in time and briefly examine how the trade fraternities of England and the trade incorporations of Scotland developed the culture of, what you and I know better as, Speculative Masonry. Time will not allow me to fully elaborate on each document or event that I cite other than to give you a brief outline of their points.

Now for reasons not known to us today, but probably because the employers of stone masons in those days were the Church, the State or local boroughs or Corporations, the trade of masons, unlike most other trades of the day, were not regulated in the same way that trades that produced and sold goods. For example, a baker purchased flour, baked bread and sold it to a consumer just in the same way a cordwainer purchased hide to make and sell shoes and so on. The mason however, was employed on site, whether it be in the quarry or the construction area, he was paid a weekly fee to produce goods for his employer, i.e. the State, Church or Borough Corporation that undertook, and could afford, to erect castles, church and bridges etc.

However, in London in 1356, we learn that:

1356

"Twelve Master Masons came before the Lord Mayor and the Aldermen at the Guildhall, London, to seek permission to draw up a simple code for trade regulation. The documents say that these men had come together because their trade had never been regulated. They ruled: '*That every man of the trade may work at any work touching the trade if he be perfectly skilled in knowing the same.*' This prevented untrained men from stealing the work of a trained man."

In the 1960s and 1970s, you may recall, we would have called that a demarcation dispute. But it was not until about 1376, that we find:

1376

"The first specific reference to a permanent organisation of Masons in London, when four masons were elected to the Common Council to represent the fellowship or mystery and the probability is that an organisation for masons was established sometime between 1356 and 1376."

Incidentally, these trade organisations that we term today as guilds were actually known as fraternities, societies or mysteries. The term mysteries relate to their trade skills and not hidden secrets regarding rites or rituals. So, in essence, we now have an organised fellowship of masons. However, in reality, the building of the Tower of London, Westminster Abbey and

London Bridge would seem to indicate that there were hundreds of stone masons working in London for the church, the State and the Corporations from about 1080 onwards, but as can be seen, it took over 300 years for them to become regulated.

It must also be pointed out at this stage that the fellowship or mystery would not have been a Lodge, as at this time the Lodge was something quite different. Often spelt *logia, logge, loygge, luge, ludge,* the word is in fact an old French Gallic word meaning hut, not in the least bit surprising when records show us that stone buildings in England were initially carried out by skilled stone workers from France. For example, in 674, Benedict Biscop brought craftsmen from Gaul to help build a stone church, in the Roman style, at Wearmouth Abbey.

The term Lodge was used to designate a mason's workshop that was generally erected in connection with any building operation. Hence, we read in the Vale Royal Abbey building accounts of 1278, carpenters were paid to erect Lodges. The same goes for mason's Lodges and workshops at Catterick Bridge in 1421, Kirby Muxloe Castle in 1481 and so on. Then we have details of repairs to mason's Lodges at Beaumaris Castle in 1330 and Westminster Abbey in 1413. Technically, the Lodge was a workshop where masons cut, dressed and carved stone and it would be fair to say that they would also have taken their permitted breaks within its walls, as recorded at the Lodge attached to York Minster in 1370 and St Giles, Edinburgh in 1491. Without a doubt and within its walls, questions affecting the masons trade were discussed like technical difficulties experienced during work, new techniques, grievances, superstitions, fables and stories passed down from mason to mason about the beginnings of the English squared stone building trade, especially in the winter months when building stopped and only carving and stone preparation took place.

In England, the formation or regulation of the stone mason's trade was marked with something else, something quite unique to English Masonic history! It coincided with the writing of the *Regius* MS *c*.1390, and the *Matthew Cooke* MS *c*.1450, both of which contain the earliest version of the charges and the legendary history of the Craft.

c.1390

The Halliwell Manuscript or Regius Poem – "In *c*.1390 we find the Halliwell Manuscript, better known to us as the Regius Poem, which is the first known Masonic text. The poem begins by talking about Euclid and his invention of geometry in ancient Egypt and then the spreading of the art of geometry in 'diver's lands'. This is followed by 15 points for the master concerning both moral behaviour and the operation of work on a building site. There are then 15 points for craftsmen which follow a similar pattern. Its author appears to have been a West of England clergyman."

1450

The Matthew Cooke Manuscript – "In 1450, we have the Matthew Cooke Manuscript which is the second oldest known manuscript in Masonic history. Typically, these Gothic Constitutions included an invocation, a mythical legend of ancient Masonry, a list of charges and regulations for Masons, and an oath or obligation. It has been dated at 1450 and it is believed to have been compiled and written in the south-eastern portion of the Western Midlands, say, in Gloucestershire or Oxfordshire, possibly also in Southeast Worcestershire or Southwest Warwickshire. The second part of the document is certainly 14th century, but the first part seems to be the beginning of the 15th. It is a copy of parts of two older manuscripts which have not survived."

Let us now turn our attention to Scotland. The first record we have of some sort of trade organisation in Scotland is found in 1474; over 100 years after the English masons were first properly regulated.

1474

The Seal of Cause – "The Seal of Cause which was granted by the Edinburgh authorities when the Masons and Wrights combined to form an incorporation, or a single association for both trades. The document gives the rules by which each trade was to be governed. Each of the trades appointed two of the best and worthiest of their craft that were sworn to search and see that the craftsmen work was lawfully done. Apprentices at the end of their terms of training were examined by four men to ensure that they were qualified to become fellow craft, if found worthy, they had to pay the requisite fee to achieve this new status. The Seal of Cause does not mention a Lodge and there is no evidence of a Lodge in Edinburgh at this period."

What this document actually shows is that there was a clear and distinct development of the mason's trade in Scotland and Scotland now had trade organisations called "incorporations" rather than fraternities or mysteries. These incorporations existed in certain Scottish burghs for the ruling and governing of particular trades. They were established, as I explained, by the "Seal of Cause" where rules and statues were made by the craftsman and approved by the municipality. In these incorporations, masons were generally associated with the wrights, however in Aberdeen in 1475 for example, a 'Seal of Cause' was granted to the coopers, wrights and masons collectively. Other incorporations which included masons were established at later dates in Glasgow, Cannongate, Lanark, Ayr, Perth, Dundee and Dumfries. But it was not until 1600 that masons were separated from, and became independent of, other trades.

In general, the role of the incorporations was the control of apprentices and the regulation of masters. They conducted periodic searches to see the work done was "sufficient and good" or "loyally and truly done". The officers were also to examine, "by an essay of craft", any person wishing to work at a trade in order to ascertain he was properly qualified. Some incorporations demanded that no craftsman was to be allowed to work on his own account until he had been admitted a burgess and freeman and like the trade associations of England, the incorporations were designed to protect the public by ensuring that the work was carried out to a standard and that the craftsman was properly qualified. However, as with or like the trade associations in England, the incorporation was not a Lodge.

Having now established the roots of what would eventually become Accepted masonry in England and non-operative masonry in Scotland, let us now examine how this developed. We have already heard that once established, the regulated masons of England began to introduce folklore and fable through the Regis and Cooke MS. However, Scotland as we know had no such documents.

The next important English document is dated 1583.

1583

"The Grand Lodge No.1 MS, of 1583, is the third oldest and is so-called because it is in possession of the United Grand

Lodge of England. It states on its face that it was "Scriptum Anno Domini 1583 Die Decembris 25. It contains its version of the history of the Craft. Also like the Regius and Cooke MSS, it contains rules of conduct of Masons. While the Regius has 15 Articles for Masters and 15 Points for Craftsmen, and the Cooke has 9 Articles for Masters and 9 Points for Fellows, the Grand Lodge No 1 MS has 9 Charges that apply to all Masons and 18 that apply specifically to Masters and Fellows."

However, 15 years later in Scotland:

1598
"On the 9 January 1598, the minutes begin for the Aitchinson Haven Lodge This was a working operative Lodge."

But, we must not get confused here! This was an operative Lodge not a non-operative Lodge, the first record of a non-operative admission was not until 1672.

Also in Scotland in 1598:

1598
The First Schaw Statutes. "On 28 December 1598 William Schaw, in his capacity of Master of Works and General Warden of the master stonemasons, issued *'The Statutis and ordinananceis to be obseruit by all the maister maoissounis within this realme.'* The preamble states that the statutes were issued with the consent of a craft convention, simply specified as all the master masons gathered that day. Schaw's first statutes root themselves in the Old Charges, with additional material to describe a hierarchy of wardens, deacons and masters. This structure would ensure that masons did not take on work which they were not competent to complete, and ensured a Lodge warden would be elected by the master masons, through whom the general warden could keep in touch with each particular Lodge. Master masons were only permitted to take on three apprentices during their lifetime (without special dispensation), and they would be bound to

their masters for seven years. A further seven years would have to elapse before they could be taken into the Craft, and a book-keeping arrangement was set up to keep track of this. Six master masons and two entered apprentices had to be present for a master or fellow of the Craft to be admitted."

1599

The Second Schaw Statutes "The Second Schaw Statutes were signed on 28 December 1599, at Holyrood house and consisted of 14 separate statutes. Some of these were addressed specifically to Lodge Mother Kilwinning, others to the Lodges of Scotland in general. Kilwinning Lodge was given regional authority for west Scotland, its previous practices were confirmed, various administrative functions were specified and the officials of the Lodge were enjoined to ensure that all Craft fellows and apprentices 'tak tryall of the art of memorie'. More generally, rules were laid down for proper record keeping of the Lodges, with specific fees being laid down. The statutes state that Kilwinning was the head and second Lodge in Scotland. This seems to relate to the fact that Kilwinning claimed precedence as the first Lodge in Scotland, but that in Schaw's scheme of things, the Edinburgh Lodge would be most important followed by Kilwinning and then Stirling."

1599

The earliest Minutes of the Lodge of Edinburgh. "Here we find the Lodge taking over the duties of the Incorporation guild/association of passing apprentices to fellow Crafts. It traces the careers of hundreds of masons in the four main stages of their working lives:

- The Apprentices at the beginning of their Indentures had to be booked in the town's Register of Apprentices.
- About three years later, they were admitted into the Lodge as entered apprentices.
- At the end of their terms, if found qualified, they were passed fellow Craft in the Lodge.
- They were now fully trained craftsmen.

In the smaller places, where there were no controls beyond those imposed by the Lodge, their status was in all respects equal to that of Master. The titles of Master and Fellow Craft were often used jointly and synonymously. In the larger towns or burghs the fellow Craft had to pass the fourth stage of Freeman-Burgess, before he could set up as Master.

However, there is still no mention of non-operative men joining the Lodge.

1600 and 1601

The Sinclair Statutes. "The two letters were drawn up in 1600 and 1601 and involved the Lodges of Dunfermline, St Andrews, Edinburgh, Aitchison's Haven and Haddington, and were signed by Schaw himself in his capacity of Master of Works (but not General Warden). They are known as the First Sinclair Statutes as they supposedly confirm the role of the lairds of Roslyn as patrons and protectors of the Craft. Once again it would suggest that Schaw's proposed reorganisation of the Craft had encountered some problems. Indeed, it presaged an ongoing struggle between the Master of Works and the Sinclairs, which Schaw's successors in the post continued, following his death in 1602."

So, between 1598 to 1601, we have Scottish records which are devoted entirely to the regulation of the operative trade which had now become the responsibility of the Lodge, rather than the incorporation, to regulate and oversee.

So to recap.
- We know that English masons sought to regulate their trade as early as 1350.
- Scotland masons were regulated over 100 years later.
- When William Shaw presented his Statutes in 1598 and 1599 power or regulation was devolved to individual or town or area Lodges.
- Scottish Lodges kept accurate records from 1598, but these only go to prove that only operative masons were permitted to be members.

- That the use of the term "Lodge" changed from that of being a site hut attached to the side of a building, to an organisation or body of masons who regulated the trade in their area.

Before we ask that all important question of which country first began the practice of admitting men by Acception or as a Non-Operative member, it may also be worthy of a mention at this stage that many trade societies, associations and fraternities accepted men not engaged in their particular craft as patrons or as a means of bestowing an honour or special privilege. It can also be said that many members of London's trade based companies, frequently came to have only a very feint connection with the business of the company to which they were attached and they included in their membership most of the wealthy men of the nation. Royal patronage of these organisations was also not uncommon as Edward III, Henry IV, Henry VI and Henry VIII were all members.

So now to ask the question, when did Lodges, north or south of the border admit non-operative masons?

I cite as my first piece of evidence the *York* MS *No 1*, which has been dated as 1600. Like the *Regius Poem* and *Matthew Cooke* MS, it contains the legendary history of the Craft and Charges for both Mason and fellows. Its provenance is claimed by an endorsement on the back of one of its pages which says. "Found in Pontifract Castle at the demolishing and given to the York Lodge by Francis Drake In 1732." Drake's father and Grandfather were both vicars of Pontefract. His grandfather was also a Royalist who was in the town when the Castle surrendered and when it was demolished in 1649. The handwriting confirms its date and what certainly marks it out as an item for more than just working craftsmen is the distinctive introduction which reads:

1600
'An Anagraime upon the name of Masonrie
William Kay to his friend Robt Preston
upon his Artt of Masonrie as Followeth:

There then follows a play on letters of the word MASONRIE.
M uch might be said of the of noble artt
A Craft that's worth esteeming in each part

> **S** undry Nations Noobles and their Kings also
> **O** h how they fought its worth to know
> **N** imrod and Solomon the wisest of all men
> **R** eason saw to love this Science then
> **I** le say no more lest by my shallow verse I
> **E** ndeavouring to praise should blemish Masonrie'

So who was William Kay and Robert Preston?

Sadly, there are no records in existence from any Lodge or group to show who this document may have belonged, but the two persons mentioned at the introduction of the MS were definitely connected with York as there are two Freemen with their names:

- William Kay was accepted as a Spurrier in 1569
- Robert Preston was accepted as a Fishmonger in 1571

If therefore these contemporaries were the actual men linked with the anagram then we have firm evidence that these persons, who were not Operative Masons, where associated with and involved in an organisation which concerned itself with 'Masonrie' and therefore become the first instance of the membership of non-operative members and what's more, their association would have begun earlier that the specified date of 1600.

So what is Scotland's reply to this?

1600

"8 June 1600. John Boswell, 3rd Laird of Auchinleck, was a Scottish gentleman and generally considered the first recorded non-operative Freemason in Scotland. Boswell's signature and mark are found on the records of a meeting of the Lodge of Edinburgh held at Holyrood on 8 June 1600."

According to many Masonic historians, this was the earliest authentic record of a non-operative Mason attending a Masonic Lodge. However, there are others who disagree. It is not clear in what capacity Boswell was in attendance at this meeting. It was not an ordinary meeting of the Lodge, but a trial of its Warden 'Jhone Broune'. While it is possible that he was there as a member (or an honorary member) of the Lodge, it is also possible that he was there only as counsel for prosecution or defence and was not a member of the Lodge at all. There is no evidence of his initiation in the

Lodge on that occasion or any other occasion, and the meeting of 8 June 1600 was the only occasion to which Boswell's connection with the this Lodge or any other can be traced.

1601

"15 April, 1601. On the west wall of the Lodge hall used by Lodge Scoon and Perth No. 3 in Perth, Scotland can be found a mural depicting James VI kneeling at their altar at his initiation. The oldest existing record of the Lodge, called '*The Mutual Agreement*' of 24 December, 1658, records that James was '*entered Freemason and Fellowcraft of the Lodge of Scoon*' on 15 April, 1601".

By the way, it was James VI that appointed William Schaw as Master of the Work and Warden General in 1583, with the commission of re-organising the Masonic Craft.

Now back in England, we have the following account of James Gilder, Mr William Warde and John Abraham Wardens of the Company of Freemasons within the City of London beginning the first day of Julie 1619 and ending the day of Julie 1620. From the entries in this book it appears that besides the ordinary Freemen and Liverymen of this Company there were other members who are termed in the books as the Accepted Masons and that they belonged to a Body known as the Accepcon or Acception

1620

"From the entries in the book of the Company of Freemasons within the City of London it appears that besides the ordinary Freemen and Liverymen of this Company there were other members who are termed in the books the Accepted Masons and that they belonged to a Body known as the Accepcon or Acception, which was an Inner Fraternity of Speculative Freemasons. Thus in the year 1620 the following entry is found: '*They charge themselves also with Money Received of the Persons hereafter named for they're gratuities at they're acceptance into the Lyvery viz*' (here follow six names). There is an entry showing sums received from several persons, of whom two are mentioned in the entry of 1620, '*Att the making masons*', and as all these mentioned were already members of *the Company something further must be meant by this.' "*

However, 14 years later in Scotland we find:

3 July 1634:
"We have the first record in Scotland of non-operative admissions which was, Lord Alexander and Sir Anthony Alexander, (both sons of the Earl of Sterling) and Sir Alexander Strachan, who were separately admitted Fellow Crafts to the Lodge of Edinburgh (St Mary's Chapel). It is thought by historian Harry Carr that they presumably received elements of the EA and FC degrees in a single session. Later minute books from the Lodge give us all the information we need to compare the steady admission of working masons with the infrequent records of non-operative masons. Despite its non-operative members, the Lodge continued to exercise its functions as an operative Lodge up to the 1700s making trade regulations for apprentices, journeyman and masters, collecting quarterages and punishing offenders."

1641
We have the first initiation in England which was conducted by members of the Lodge of Edinburgh (Mary's Chapel) on 20 May 1641 at Newcastle when Sir Robert Moray was made a Mason.

1642
The minutes begin at Kilwinning Lodge although the records for the admission of nobility and gentry as non-operatives do not begin until 1672.

1646
The Diary of Elias Ashmole tells us that he was made a Freemason *"at Warrington in Lancashire, with Colonel Henry Mainwaring of Cheshire; the other names of those that were in attendance at the Lodge were: Richard Penkett, James Collier, Richard Sankey, Henry Littler, John Ellam. Richard Ellam and Hugh Brewer"*.

Incidentally, none of the above mentioned names had anything to do with the building trade. They were all members of the local gentry.

1660

Randal Holme, III who died in 1700, left a paper containing the names of 26 brethren, all members of the Old Lodge at Chester for about the year 1660. Research has shown that of those 26 members, at least 16 were not operative masons as six were Mayors or Aldermen, eight were Freeman of the Town, one was a Churchwarden and one was the son of an MP.

1670

The earliest Lodge records in Aberdeen begin. A list shows there were 10 operative master masons or fellow crafts on the roll and 39 non-operatives, drawn from the nobility, gentry, professional men, merchants and tradesmen.

1672

The minutes of the Aitchinson Haven Lodge which was an operative Lodge record their first non-operative admission.

1682

Elias Ashmole records a further diary entry which says, "About 5 P.M. I received a Summons to appear at a Lodge to be held next day, at Masons Hall London."

Interestingly, of the 15 present that evening, one was an antiquarian, three were contractors whose named are associated with the building of St Pauls, one was a chief importer of stone into London, eight were members of the London Company of Masons of which three were part of the Livery of the Company and four were part of the Court of Assistants of the Company.

1701

The minutes of the operative Lodge at Alnwick (Northumberland) begin. These are the earliest records of an English Lodge to survive. They begin with a code of operative and moral regulations. They styled themselves "The Company and Fellowship of Free Masons" and met as a Lodge and all men admitted were operative masons."

1702
The Lodge at Haughfoot becomes what was the first wholly non-operative Scottish Lodge.

Crucially, a member of that Lodge, probably the first secretary, wrote in the first several pages of the first minute book, the complete admission procedure of that period. Sometime later, a well-meaning brother tore out the pages so as not to reveal to any unauthorised person the details of the ritual or ceremony. However, the last 29 words of the ceremony were left at the top of the page with the heading underneath *"The same day"* with the start of the minutes of the Lodge. The 29 words were authentic ritual and verified three other important documents which up until the discovery of the minute book of the Lodge could not be verified as authentic. The documents are, the Edinburgh Register House MS 1696, the Chetwode Crawley MS *c.*1700, the Kevan MS *c.*1714. The fragment provided the all-important link to a ritual that was believed to have been practised the previous 50–100 years.

So there you have it Brethren, placed before you are the relevant records and dates that have been available to me at the time of putting this lecture together. They are subject to change if other records come to light. I will leave it to you to determine which country admitted the first non-operative mason to its membership, but at this stage the pendulum has swung in favour of England.

To conclude this evenings presentation, I will add a couple of other dates which complete the time line:

1717
In London, we find recorded the establishment of the first Grand Lodge, however, initially this was set up for the area of Westminster only, not the whole of England.

1730
Thanks to an exposure of the day, this date marks the first year when the term "Degree" was used to describe the three parts of the Craft, ie, Entered Apprentice Degree.

1736

This year marks the formation of the Grand Lodge of Scotland.

1757

Is the first date that I can find that the term "Speculative" was used to describe Gentleman or Accepted Masons.

Postscript

It would be very remiss of me that if reading through this book and reaching this Postscript I had not offered you my thanks. Therefore, I greet you all right well and send you my hearty good wishes in the hope that the book has broadened your Masonic understanding, prompted you to question our practices and seek out their origins or better still put pen to paper, or rather, more likely than not, fingers to keyboard, and start to write yourself.

When I became a Freemason in 1994, other than the sheer excitement we all feel and the anticipation of not knowing what will happen next, the night passed off very quickly. The whole evening went off well with a lot of back-slapping, toasting and general merriment. In fact, it was a while before I realised that Freemasonry was a lot more than a jolly boys club. My epiphany came the day somebody asked me in all innocence, "So what do you Freemasons do?" My Masonic immaturity and my lack of knowledge meant that I blustered out some unsatisfactory answer and changed the subject quickly. This no doubt left a genuine question unanswered and the natural inquisitiveness of the individual void of any adequate substance to quell his curiosity. I vowed never to allow myself to be put it that position again and at that point I felt I truly started my Masonic career.

Whatever way you look at it, Freemasonry is a journey of which there are many metaphorical crossroads along the way. Some lead Freemasons to make a Masonic career out of joining as many side or appendant degrees as possible, some make a career out of supporting their Lodge by their attendance at its meetings, Festive Boards and Ladies Nights, while others are content to ignore those diversions and do neither, they join, they are happy attend to their basic Lodge duties, but are reticent to commit or take Office or deviate from the single straight road, but there should not be any criticism whatsoever attached to any path a Freemason decides to take.

My journey through Freemasonry seemed to be entirely different to any other Freemason I know. I was never one to collect degrees, I never had to be seen at Ladies' nights, charity bashes or Provincial functions, in fact I experienced a period in my Masonic career, which I now refer to as my "wilderness years". Through a series of personal issues, I left my mother Lodge and Chapter and spent about eight years researching, writing, and lecturing (of which all the proceeds went to various charities) on Freemasonry. I was also employed as the Manager of a Masonic Centre and during those years I was also Tyler to five Craft and one Mark Lodge and Janitor to two Chapters, so I was fully engaged in Masonic activity, but not involved in one single Lodge. That self-appointed exile from my mother Lodge and Chapter developed a resilience in me to ensure I spread the Masonic word and participate, where I could, in the education of our people. I came in from the cold after receiving an Active Provincial Appointment and the honour of presenting the Annual Cornwallis Lecture. From that point on I re-invented or refreshed my approach and continued to research, write and lecture with a greater intensity, the culmination of some of that work manifests itself in this book.

If there is one single thing that I believe Freemasonry lacks, it is not giving any single direction to educating our members. To a certain point I can understand that with a questionable origin, a variety of rituals and no one single answer to any question, we are all stumbling in the dark. But there are answers to those questions, there are plausible explanations and there are early documents to substantiate historical facts. So, where are they, I here everybody asking. Well they are all there, but the onus is on the individual to find them, this book being the living example of that fact. All I have done over the years is to read, note and collate other people's work and present them with my own interpretation. I think we all realise that to repeat one source is plagiarism, however two or more sources become *bona fide* research and after all, there is no point reinventing the wheel.

If I have learnt one thing from the many hundreds of lectures I have given, the thousands of Brethren I have met and the many questions I have been asked, is that Brethren have a thirst for knowledge, but they do know where to look. I always saw my role as one of tipping information into a sieve, which then filters into a funnel and the result being a lecture on the subject in hand. Fortunately, the by-product of the sieve is that the information not used is not wasted, but stored for another project. Therefore,

I was always one lecture ahead of myself with ideas, notes and subject matter.

The point I am making is that you do have to lead the horse to water, we do have to drip-fed our members with good solid information. Information they can take away, absorb, consider, formulate, understand and add to their foundation of Masonic knowledge. This process will then ensure the future of our Craft is safe, that the fundamental ethos is not allowed to die and Freemasonry, in all its splendour, will continue for the next 300 years.

Index